OVERCOMING LONELINESS

OVERCOMING LONELINESS

by

David Jeremiah

HERE'S LIFE PUBLISHERS, INC.
San Bernardino, California 92402

OVERCOMING LONELINESS
by David Jeremiah

Published by
HERE'S LIFE PUBLISHERS, INC.
P.O. Box 1576
San Bernardino, CA 92402

Library of Congress Catalog Card 83-048411
ISBN 0-89840-049-X
HLP Product No. 95-055-0

PRINTED IN THE UNITED STATES OF AMERICA.

Scripture quotations are from the King James Version (The Open Bible) except for those designated NIV, which are quoted from the New International Version, published by Zondervan Publishing House, Grand Rapids, Michigan.

To our special friends who constantly have encouraged us: Bill and Dottie Vanderford and Swen and Marlene Nater.

Acknowledgments

My heartfelt thanks to Sally Wolff who diligently typed the original manuscript . . . to Virginia Hearn who so sensitively edited the chapters . . . and to Les Stobbe who heard me preach on the subject of loneliness and encouraged me to put this material in print. Most of all, to Donna, my life's partner, best friend, and number one cheerleader.

Contents

Loneliness— Disease of the Decade

Chapter One

Loneliness—Disease of the Decade

Loneliness may well be the disease of the decade, perhaps of every decade in our mid and late twentieth century. An early sociological study of loneliness, *The Lonely Crowd,* came out in the early 1950s. "They are crammed and jammed in buses," a modern poet wrote, "but each of them's alone."

"Too strong," you say. Well, "A fourth of the people questioned in one survey said they felt very lonely or cut off from other people at some time during the preceding few weeks. In another study, 27 percent of the unmarried women (plus 10 percent of the married women) and 23 percent of the unmarried men (plus 6 percent of the married men) expressed intense loneliness. Almost half the widows over fifty living in one large metropolitan area said that loneliness was their worst problem. Loneliest of all, researchers find, are elderly men, who live alone and are infirm" (Craig W. Ellison, "Roots of Loneliness," *Christianity Today,* 1978).

Social isolation, the sudden loss of love, and chronic loneliness contributes significantly to illness and even to premature death.

An interviewee in *People* magazine was asked the connection between loneliness and health. "That's like asking 'What is the connection between *air* and one's health?' " he replied. Like the air we breathe, we take human companionship for granted until we're deprived of it. Loneliness, isolation from others, takes a tremendous toll in people's lives.

What is loneliness? Some describe it in physical terms. It's an empty feeling in the pit of one's stomach, almost to the point of nausea. Others describe it as an underlying anxiety, "a big black pit." Some say loneliness is a sharp ache in moments of grief or separation. For others it's a long period of stress that wears them down until they're discouraged and defeated.

In a recent article on loneliness, Katherine Barrett comments: "In a society where most people live in impersonal cities or suburbs, where electronic entertainment often replaces one-to-one conversation, where people move from job to job, and state to state, and marriage to marriage, loneliness has become an epidemic" (Katherine Barrett, *Ladies Home Journal,* May, 1983, p. 90).

There is no anguish like the anguish of loneliness. I read it in the letters that come to my desk from prisoners behind bars. I hear it in the voice of a woman who calls me on the phone to tell me that her husband has left her. I watch it in the face of a husband who has just buried his wife. I ache with its effects as I hug grandparents and parents at the funeral of a beautiful child who was snatched from their presence in just a few hours by a violent disease.

I observe the cruelty of it in the faces of single people who are trying to find community and fellowship in a religious and social world that is family-oriented and couple-centered. I see it in teenagers who are moving through the transition from children to adulthood in that unexplainable time when everything is changing; they feel their parents don't understand; they're all alone to experience this strangeness. I see it in the eyes of my wife when the ministry to which God has called us separates us for many nights in a row.

I listen to the music of loneliness on the radio. Music like "Without You," "I'm So Lonely I Could Die," "Ballad of a Lonely Man," and

"All the lonely people—where do they all come from?"

Do you remember learning *The Rime of the Ancient Mariner* in school?

> Alone, alone, all all alone,
> Alone on a wide, wide sea!
> And never a saint took pity on
> My soul in agony.

The lives of thousands of people are summarized by that poem. As David said in the psalms, "No one cares for my soul" (Psalm 142:4).

In his book *The Devil's Advocate,* Morris West writes: "Let me tell you something important. It is no new thing to be lonely. It comes to all of us sooner or later. Friends die, family dies, lovers and husbands, too. We get old, we get sick. The last and greatest loneliness is death. There are no pills to cure that. There are no formulas to make it go away. It is a [human] condition we cannot escape, and if we try to run from it we are driven to a darker hell than the one we experience in the midst of it. But if we face it we remember that there are a million others like us and if we reach out to comfort *them* and not ourselves, we discover in the end that we are lonely no longer, for we are in a new family, the family of man" (Morris L. West,

The Devil's Advocate, New York: Dell, 1959, pp. 334-335).

As Christians, I believe we can go one step further. Not only are we in the family of men, we are in the family of God. We have the reassurance that God wants to meet us in our loneliness and we find that, with His help, we can overcome it.

Lonely
Saints

A Psalm in a Hotel Room

I'm alone Lord
alone
a thousand miles from home.
There's no one here who knows my name
except the clerk
and he spelled it wrong,
no one to eat dinner with
laugh at my jokes
listen to my gripes
be happy with me about what happened
today
and say that's great.
No one cares.
There's just this lousy bed
and slush in the street outside
between the buildings.
I feel sorry for myself
and I've plenty of reason to.
Maybe I ought to say
I'm on top of it
praise the Lord
things are great
but they're not.
Tonight
it's all
gray slush.

—Joseph Bayly
(Psalms of My Life
Wheaton, Il: Tyndale House Pubs., 1969)

Chapter Two

Lonely Saints

Every year during football season a lot of Americans spend many enjoyable hours with their favorite team. And then it's over. It's gone. That's a picture of life, isn't it? The things that have no eternal value, but are just temporal—they go, they end, and a kind of emptiness is there when it's all over.

The things of eternal value don't leave you with that feeling. It isn't like that in our relationship with the Lord. There we find rest and joy and happiness in Jesus Christ, and not in whether or not something happens, or whether our team wins.

People face different kinds of loneliness. There is a kind of loneliness that comes to us when we lose a loved one. That kind touches us at the deepest core of our life. Some readers of this book in the past year have lost someone in their immediate family—a husband, wife, child, grandparent—and there's an aching loneliness in their hearts because of that.

There's a kind of loneliness that comes from being away from your friends. Missionaries often speak of that. They know what it's like to be on the other side of the world, facing crises, with nobody there to help. Nobody is close enough to you to understand what you're experiencing.

Another kind of loneliness can take place when you're with others—in the midst of a large crowd, or when you're surrounded even by people you love.

Christians sometimes are called to take positions that are unpopular, that do not meet with the approval of the majority. We feel very much alone then, and because of that experience we can identify with a man in the Bible who for fifty years carried on a public ministry that was unappreciated.

Jeremiah the prophet, through the reign of five different kings, watched terrible things happen to the people whom God had called him to minister to. The first few verses of his prophecy, the book of Jeremiah in the Old Testament, listed the three main kings under whom he served: Josiah, Jehoiakim, and Zedekiah. Along with those three were two other kings who served only three-month reigns. He watched disorder on a national level because of that political upheaval and corrupt leadership. He saw disturbing social problems all around him. He saw dissensions tear his people apart inwardly. Discontent and despair seemed to be the mood of his generation. But he kept on ministering as a prophet of God in the land of Judah, however unpopular, opposed, condemned, ridiculed, and scorned he was.

On one occasion he was stoned, thrown out of his home town. On another occasion he was beaten up in public disgrace. Another time he was imprisoned, and once he was thrown into a pit and left there for dead. Eventually he wrote a whole book of what we might call funeral poems. They were his outpourings of grief at the destruction of the holy city. He has been called the "weeping prophet." We call that book The Lamentations of Jeremiah. If you haven't read it recently, read it and you'll get a picture of a lonely, hurting man.

Jeremiah ministered during the last years of Judah's history, from the thirteenth year of King Josiah until the destruction of the nation. The decline of his nation depressed him. He said: "A horrible and shocking thing has happened in the land: The prophets prophesy lies, the priests rule by their own authority, and my people love it this way" (Jeremiah 5:30,31).

The prophets were not speaking from God, the priests were using their sacred office for personal gain, and the people didn't object. That kind of corruption was to their fancy. Jeremiah looked out over his nation and saw a whole generation of backslidden people. They had fallen away from their godly moorings. They had walked a road away from God. "The harvest is past, the summer has ended, and we are not saved" (Jeremiah 8:20). As he looked at the awful apathy among the people who were supposed to be God's people, depression swept into his soul.

One of the key words in this book is the word *backslide.* You may have thought it was just a Baptist term, but now you know it goes all the way back to the book of Jeremiah. Over and over again, this book talks about God's people being backslidden in condition.

> Thine own wickedness shall correct thee, and thy backsliding shall reprove thee: know therefore and see that it is an evil thing and bitter... (2:19).
>
> The Lord said also unto me in the days of Josiah the king, Hast thou seen that which backsliding Israel hath done? (3:6).
>
> And I saw, when for all the causes whereby backsliding Israel committed adultery I had put her away... (3:8).

> Return, ye backsliding children, and I will heal your backslidings (3:22).

Jeremiah cried out against all this, but his cries fell on deaf ears.

Years ago, a British historian wrote these words about another man, yet they could easily apply to Jeremiah the prophet. "It is difficult to conceive any situation more painful than that of a great man, condemned to watch the lingering agony of an exhausted country, to tend it during the alternating fits of stupefaction and raving which precede its dissolution, and to see the symptoms of vitality disappear one by one until nothing is left but coldness and darkness and corruption."

That's what happened to Jeremiah. He stood in the nation he loved, among the people to whom God had called him, and watched its awful moral decline that ultimately ended up in captivity. Jeremiah went to his grave having seen the death of his nation.

It is one thing to watch a nation fall—it's another thing to watch its people be totally insensitive to the inevitable. Jeremiah's heart was broken by that kind of disinterest. You could write over the generation of his day the words *apathy* and *indifference*. Jeremiah wept about their sad spiritual state. He spent a lot of time in tears.

> Oh that my head were waters, and mine eyes a fountain of tears, that I might

> weep day and night for the slain of the daughter of my people! (9:1).
>
> But if ye will not hear it, my soul shall weep in secret places for your pride... (13:17).
>
> Let mine eyes run down with tears night and day, and let them not cease: for the virgin daughter of my pepole is broken with a great breach, with a very grievous blow (14:17).

In the book of Lamentations we see reference after reference as Jeremiah poured out his tears for a nation that had been reared on the precepts of God and had turned from them. Now God had raised him up, a prophet who came to pronounce God's judgment and the way of deliverance, and they did not listen. Their ears were closed. They refused to hear. As Jeremiah thought about that in the night watches, loneliness swept into his soul. He stood alone as God's representative in a decadent society.

Jeremiah was also distressed by the desertion of his friends. "Behold, O Lord; for I am in distress: my heart is troubled... They have heard that I sigh; there is none to comfort me: all mine enemies have heard of my trouble; they are glad that thou hast done it..." (Lamentations 1:20,21)

That's why he could write these words: "I sat not in the assembly of the mockers, nor rejoiced; I sat alone because of thy hand: for thou hast filled me with indignation. Why is my pain perpetual, and my wound incurable, which refuseth to be healed?" (Jeremiah 15:17,18).

We see how Jeremiah felt what all of us are prone to feel in such situations. He was ready to disown it all. He had what we call in the modern vernacular his own private pity party. And thinking back over what we've already learned about this lonely man, we cannot really blame him that from the human standpoint he wanted to die. He came to the place where he was ready to quit. He was all by himself, and you can feel the ache of his heart as he writes. All of us at one time or another know how that feels. I don't know what it was that finally was the last blow, but one day Jeremiah woke up and decided it was too much for him.

> Cursed be the day on which I was born: let not the day on which my mother bore me be blessed. Cursed be the man who brought tidings to my father, saying, A male child is born unto thee; making him very glad. And let that man be as the cities which the Lord overthrew, and repented not: and let him hear the cry in the morning, and the shouting at noontide; Because he slew me not from the womb; or that my mother might have been my grave, and her womb to be

> always great with me. Why came I forth out of the womb to see labor and sorrow, that my days should be consumed with shame? (Jeremiah 20:14-18).

Jeremiah said, "I regret the day of my birth. Don't ever mention my birthday again. I wish I hadn't been born. And the man who came down to the father's room from the maternity ward to say to him that his child has been born—well, cursed be the messenger of my birth!"

That's how low he was. Jeremiah had hit bottom. He didn't want to go on. Someone (I don't know who) took time to write a paraphrase of that particular passage of Scripture. A paraphrase like this, written by a modern-day pastor, had to have been written on Monday morning. This is how it goes: "I had no idea when You called me into Your service that it would be like this. I pictured myself preaching great sermons, perhaps working a miracle now and then. I foresaw some opposition, but I thought I would override it in calm victory. You never mentioned my destruction, or the number of those who would despise me. You neglected to mention that everyone in Jerusalem would mock me constantly. I'm the laughing stock of all Judah! Everyone points or smirks or laughs or snarls at me when I walk down the street, even the smallest children. I quit!"

Do you ever talk like that? "I quit!" That was where Jeremiah was. He wanted to disown the whole thing. Everyone at one time or another has thought the way he did then. "Oh, that I had in the wilderness a lodging place of wayfaring men; that I might leave my people, and go from them! for they are all adulterers, an assembly of treacherous men" (Jeremiah 9:2).

What was he saying? "I wish I had a Motel 6 in the wilderness so that I could get away from all this hassle. If I did, I'd do it tomorrow. If I could just get in my car and drive away from it all, leave it behind me, oh, what a good feeling that would be!"

Do you ever feel like that? James Conway, in *Men in Mid-Life Crisis,* talks about how he sometimes feels as a pastor, husband and father. "I feel like a vending machine, dispensing products. Someone pushes a button, and out comes a sermon. Someone pushes another button for a solution to a personal or administrative problem. The family pushes buttons, and out comes dollars or time involvement. The community pushes other buttons, and I show up at meetings, sign petitions, and take stands. It is easy for a man...to feel that he is trapped with obligations to everyone, and the frustration is that he can't get out" (Jim Conway, *Mid-Life*

Crisis, Elgin, IL: David C. Cook Publishing Co., 1978, p. 57).

Jeremiah was ready to cut out, but he didn't do it. For fifty years he stayed by the stuff, so to speak, unappreciated. Nobody gave him applause. Nobody came by and said, "Boy, that's tremendous what you're doing to save our nation." Yet even though he had his low moments, he was faithful to what God called him to do. He didn't throw in the towel.

I'm glad the Bible has recorded his emotions. Doesn't that make you feel better? To know that a man in the Word of God had those emotions. Sometimes people say that the Bible paints plastic men, straw people, but it doesn't. It paints them the way they are. Real flesh and blood individuals whose feelings sound a lot like ours.

What he did, you and I can do. The things that were true in his life can be true in our lives. How did he do it? Four stabilizing factors kept Jeremiah secure, kept him at the task to which God had called him. Four concrete principles caused him to be victorious.

First, he had a conviction of his calling. Did I say *conviction?* Well, at first he said, "Okay, it seems like no matter what I do, whenever I open my mouth, somebody doesn't like it. I'll tell you what—I'm not even going to talk. I'll just be quiet. I know when to shut up. I won't even mention the Lord's name." That's what he thought about doing. "Then I said, I will not make mention of Him, nor speak any more in His name. But His word was in mine heart as a burning fire shut up in my bones, and I was weary with forbearing, and I could not refrain" (Jeremiah 20:9).

Jeremiah said, "I wanted just to keep quiet about God, not even speak His name any more. But when I tried to keep silent, God's Word was like a fire burning in my bones. That fire had to be released."

You ask, "Where in the world did he get such conviction?" Well, in his life it came with the realization that he was a man to whom the call of God had come. If you go back to the first chapter, you will understand why that call was such an important part of his life. "Then the word of the Lord came unto me, saying, Before I formed thee in the womb I knew thee; and before thou camest forth out of the womb I sanctified thee, and I ordained thee a prophet unto the nations" (Jeremiah 1:4,5).

We notice four things in that verse about his calling. God said, "Jeremiah, I *knew* you before you were formed. I *formed* you in the womb. I *sanctified* you, set you apart for my service. I *ordained* you; you're my man; you do it."

Do you know what the name *Jeremiah*

means? Literally it means "whom Jehovah appoints." Jeremiah realized that he was an appointed servant. He was called by God. In the midst of the discouragements of his life and the problems of his society, the thing that held him in there was the realization that he was where God wanted him to be. He was doing what God wanted him to do. Though he didn't understand the circumstances, that was enough for him.

When I was considering going in the ministry, one day my father said, "David, if you can do anything else, do it." That was rather strange advice for a man to give his son, I thought, when I knew he'd been praying all his life that I'd be a preacher. What he meant was this: "If your call to the ministry is not so strong as to blot out your desire for any other vocation, when trouble comes, you'll vacillate. You'll want to skip out." It can't be just a professional thing.

To be a man or woman of God in this world today, you must be sure of your calling. That has nothing to do with being a pastor. For instance, some of you may be college students who are facing financial stress and academic pressure. You could be thinking about how great it would be to have a job where you earned money and could do the things you want to do. The pressure is on and you want to quit. But if you really believe that God called you to go to school, you won't do that.

Every person has a calling from God, every one of you. Whatever it is, you'd better be sure of it. If you know that's where God has put you, it'll help you when tough times come.

So reason number one for Jeremiah's steadfastness when he wanted to quit was his conviction of his calling. He wanted to get out but something in him drove him onward. That something was the fact that God had put him in that place, given him a job to do, implanted His word in him.

Second, Jeremiah had confidence in his companion.

> For I heard the defaming of many, fear on every side. Report, say they, and we will report it. All my friends watched for my fall, saying, Perhaps he will be enticed, and we shall prevail against him, and we shall take our revenge on him. *But the Lord is with me as a mighty terrible one:* therefore my persecutors shall stumble, and they shall not prevail (Jeremiah 20:10,11, italics mine).

Jeremiah said, "I know they're after me. I know even my friends are trying to get me. But I've got the Lord, and He's my companion." Do you remember what Jeremiah had said when God asked him to go into the ministry? He said, "Lord, I can't do that. I'm a child. I'm not mature enough."

The Lord answered his objection with these words: "Be not afraid of their faces: for I am with thee to deliver thee" (Jeremiah 1:8). "And they shall fight against thee; but they shall not prevail against thee; for I am with thee" (verse 19).

I don't believe all those trite sayings that are often passed off on people who experience loneliness—for instance, that you don't need anybody but Jesus. I know better than that. We need companionship. We need fellowship. That's something that God has built into us. But in those moments when we are between friends, in those dark caverns of being all alone, we have a Companion who stays with us through it all.

> But now thus saith the Lord that created thee, O Jacob, and he that formed thee, O Israel, Fear not: for I have redeemed thee, I have called thee by thy name; thou art mine. When thou passest through the waters, I will be with thee; and through the rivers, they shall not overflow thee; when thou walkest through the fire, thou shalt not be burned; neither shall the flame kindle upon thee. For I am the Lord thy God, the Holy One of Israel, thy Savior" (Isaiah 43:1-3).

Third, Jeremiah had a commitment that went beyond his circumstances. "Blessed is the person who trusteth in the Lord, and whose hope the Lord is. For he shall be as a tree planted by the waters, and that spreadeth out her roots by the river, and shall not see when heat cometh, but her leaf shall be green; and shall not be anxious in the year of drought, neither shall cease from yielding fruit'' (Jeremiah 17:7).

Jeremiah was saying, ''When you put your roots down deep in trust in God, when your faith is in Him, your confidence goes beyond the circumstances.'' How many Christians' faith vacillates with the circumstances. But Jeremiah said, "In the midst of all these problems and troubles and difficulties, my trust is in the Lord. It doesn't matter whether it's summer or winter or what. I don't need to be anxious because I have a commitment beyond these circumstances."

Do you have that? Or are you in that everyday hassle that so many people experience, up and down, up and down, in reaction to their circumstances?

Faith says, ''Be not weary in well doing: for in due season we shall reap if we faint not'' (Galatians 6:9). Faith says, ''He that goeth forth and weepeth, bearing precious seed, shall doubtless come again with rejoicing bringing his sheaves with him'' (Psalm 126:6). Faith says, ''Be ye steadfast, unmovable, always abounding in the work of the Lord, forasmuch as ye know that your labor is not in vain in the Lord'' (1 Corinthians 15:58). Someone has said, "Integrity is carrying out a commitment after the environment in which the commitment was made has dissipated.''

Fourth, Jeremiah had a chorus of celebration. "Sing unto the Lord, praise ye the Lord: for he hath delivered the soul of the poor from the hand of evildoers'' (Jeremiah 20:13). You say, "How in the world can a person in a situation like Jeremiah's sing to the Lord?'' He did it by faith.

Doctors talk about the threshold of pain, the level at which you experience pain. Some people have a high threshold. Others have a very low threshold. When you take an aspirin, that has nothing to do with your problem physically. All it does is raise the threshold of pain, so that you don't feel pain at such a low level. It makes you feel better because you don't feel how bad you feel. Joy is like that. Happiness and joy are like spiritual aspirin. When you are filled with the joy of the Lord, the hurts around you don't touch you quite so quickly.

I have found that music also literally raises the threshold of pain in my life. On days when I am discouraged I'll go home, turn on the stereo, begin to listen to music, and God uses that to assuage my soul and bring me up out of pain. Is it any wonder that Saul required David to come and play on his harp and bring him out of his depression? That's what music can do in our hearts.

Do you know what is being established medically now? Joy raises the threshold of pain. A book by Norman Cousins called *The Anatomy of an Illness As Perceived by the Patient* has been on the bestseller list; it's just delightful. Cousins was told he had one chance in five hundred to live. So he secured some old "Candid Camera" shows along with other humorous films and he began to watch those comedies every two hours from morning till night. And you know what? He started to get better (Norman Cousins, *The Anatomy of an Illness As Perceived by the Patient*, New York and London: W. W. Horton and Co., Inc., 1979, pp 39,40).

In effect he said, "If I'm going to die, I don't want to die in surroundings like this." He left the hospital and rented a hotel room, a plush hotel room, and started laughing. He demonstrated the truth of the Old Testament statement that says, "A merry heart doeth good like a medicine." Many times, the joy of praise and thanksgiving to God will dissipate the hurt you feel.

When Ezra was conducting a revival during the days of Nehemiah, he gave his people a great truth. "The joy of the Lord is your strength" (Nehemiah 8:10).

Are you joyful? Do you have anything you're praising God for? I learned a long time ago that there is always something for which I can give thanks. On the very worst day I still can be glad about something.

While I was on vacation this summer, I read a feature story on the death of Otto Frank, the father of Anne Frank. (*The Diary of Anne Frank* has been put on as a play in almost every school in the country, I suspect.) The article talked about the hardships and difficulties the family experienced during that awful holocaust, when they were prisoners in their own house for over three years. A section was quoted from the diary of Anne Frank, written in 1944 when she was a young girl. "Nearly every evening I go to the attic, and from my favorite spot on the floor, I look up at the blue sky. As long as this exists, I thought, and I may live to see it—this sunshine, the cloudless skies—while this lasts, I cannot be unhappy. Riches can all be lost, but that happiness in your own heart can only be veiled."

We have something more than blue sky and clouds. We have Jesus Christ living in us.

Though the world may crumble around us, He is the blue sky, He is the light from on high that thrills and encourages our hearts. I can look beyond the circumstances into the face of the one who loves me more than I know, one who would never allow me to go through anything that is not for my own good. And I say to myself, and to you, *Don't quit.*

Lonely
Singles

Oh, Father I just need a reason to go on.
It's gettin' dark, Father. I'm afraid. This
reminds me of another dark place I knew;
I was three years stumbling through it.
Not again, Father, please!
I hurt. Inside I am screaming. I do not
want this. One by one You have taken
away the people I depended on. Now only
You are left. I do not want to trust You—
You Who have taken away all that
mattered. But I am too tired to fight You
anymore.
Would You hold my hand, please? It's
getting darker. Too dark now to see more
than a step ahead. And colder too.
You know, You don't talk to me like
people do. I guess that's what I miss. And
people are tangible. I can feel them there.

It's all black now, Father. It looks to me
like it will never be bright again. Not
here. But when we get to Your place,
that's bright again isn't it?

It's hard to accept this blackness for that long. But I guess You're not asking me to. Only to accept it for now, this present minute. It's just that these minutes run together 'til I can hardly remember a time before them...

(Debbie Armstrong, "For Heaven's Sake," *Insight Series ABWE*, Cherry Hill, NJ: Association of Baptists for World Evangelism, Inc., 1982, p. 17) Used by Permission

I was born again as a result of being divorced so I praise the Lord for my divorce. I try to be a blessing, but I am so lonely. Sometimes you get tired of giving, of hurting, and you just want to talk and fit in. As for fitting in, forget it. No one understands because they are couple-oriented. How could they? Help!

I'm so confused in my thoughts and hurting on the inside so bad I think I'll burst. I'm a thirty-seven-year-old woman whose husband left her with four children.

I've prayed and I'm trying so hard to put my problems in God's hand and leave them alone, but it's so hard. I know I'm full of bitterness and resentfulness. But I'm so lonely. I don't have anyone to talk to or any place to go for help.

I am so tired from trying to keep this going. Sometimes I feel that if I could get sick and die, then God would have to take the kids and I wouldn't have to worry anymore. I realize I need counseling, but I can't afford it. I cry every night and pray myself to sleep. I've always tried to be a good person and can't understand why this is happening. I'm trying to keep my faith like Job in the Bible, but I just don't know how much more I can take.

I was happily married for twenty-four years and praise God for those years. I've been single for five years now (not by choice), but I hadn't thought of it as a "blessing" until you brought it to my attention. Why is it a blessing? Because I have been closer to the Lord than ever before in my life.

Chapter Three

Lonely Singles

One of the great phenomena of our day is the "singles explosion" in our country. Between 1970 and 1982, their ranks swelled from 10.9 million to 19.4 million, a 78 percent jump. Almost a third of those living alone have never been married. Their ranks grew from 2.8 million to almost 6 million between 1970 and 1981. According to the *U.S. News and World Report,* the number of Americans living alone has increased 385 percent between 1950 and 1982 *(U.S. News and World Report,* Feb. 21, 1983, pp. 53,54).

A staggering one in seven American children is raised by a single parent. In urban areas, that number is one in four. If we include all the different kinds of single people (for example, the widowed and divorced), we must acknowledge that there are 50 million single people in the United States. Today one-fifth of all households in the United States consist of a person living alone.

The real estate industry has reacted to that phenomenon by building a growing number of condominiums for singles only. Smaller houses are being built, with fewer rooms, reflecting the needs of our single population. Someone has estimated that singles have a purchasing power of 60 billion dollars per year.

The need for satisfying relationships on the part of single people has caused all kinds of new enterprises to grow up: singles' bars, encounter and support groups, computerized dating services. A Christian newspaper carried an ad beginning like this: "God did not ordain singleness and loneliness." The ad urged singles to subscribe to a monthly publication through which they could meet other singles on four continents.

One older woman put it this way: "I sit in the pew next to a warm body every week, but I feel no heat. I'm in the faith, but I draw no active love. I sing the hymns with those next to me, but I hear only my own voice. When the service is finished, I leave as I came in—hungry for someone to touch me, to tell me that I'm a person worth something to somebody. Just a smile would do it, or perhaps some gesture, some sign that I am not a stranger."

Have you read Ann Kiemel's books? She is a contemporary young woman who has written about being single. In *I Love the Word Im-*

possible she includes a prayer she prayed when she was single and all alone on a New Year's Eve.

God,
it's new year's eve
and i took a hot bath
and poured powder and lotion
and perfume recklessly,
and donned
my newest
long, dainty
nightgown.
i guess i was hoping
all that would erase
the agony
of being
alone
in such a gallant,
celebrating,
profound moment
when everyone so likes
to be with someone
to watch
a new year in.
it hasn't helped
too much.
i've tried to sleep
hoping that would beat
away the endless hours, but
after all afternoon and two hours
tonight, i'm worn out from sleep.
i've stumbled from one room
to the next,
wanting to cry. . .
o God,

the walls are so silent...
and there is no one around
to laugh and
change the subject...
i so wish for a friend's lap,
to bury my head
and let my tears spill
unabashedly and free...

From *I Love the Word Impossible*, by Ann Kiemel, Published by Tyndale House Publishers, Inc.,© 1976, pp. 136,138). Used by permission.

One day I walked into our singles class and I asked them to write me a letter expressing the difficulties in the single life. Their letters were a revelation. In 1 Corinthians we learn that God is not confused (as a lot of us are) about this subject.

> Now for the matters you wrote about: It is good for a man not to marry.
>
> I wish that all men were as I am. But each man has his own gift from God; one has this gift, another has that.
>
> Now to the unmarried and the widows I say: It is good for them to stay unmarried, as I am. But if they cannot control themselves, they should marry, for it is better to marry than to burn with passion.
>
> I would like you to be free from concern. An unmarried man is concerned about the Lord's affairs—how he can please the Lord. But a married man is concerned

> about the affairs of this world—how he can please his wife—and his interests are divided. An unmarried woman or virgin is concerned about the Lord's affairs: Her aim is to be devoted to the Lord in both body and spirit. But a married woman is concerned about the affairs of this world—how she can please her husband. I am saying this for your own good, not to restrict you, but that you may live in a right way in undivided devotion to the Lord (1 Corinthians 7:1, 7-9, 32-35, NIV).

I believe that God says five things to singles. First, *acknowledge your singleness.* Three times in 1 Corinthians 7 we read "It is good" (verses 1, 8, 26). Why is that so startling? Well, most singles have been made to feel that to be single is to be second class. Let a letter express it for me.

> Dear Pastor:
>
> I too am single—never been married—and I really believe some couples and elderly people don't realize the hurt and grief they sometimes inflict on us. I often get questions and comments like these: "What's a sweet girl like you doing single?" "God has just the right man somewhere." "Maybe a friend's wife will die!" "What's wrong with you?" "When are you getting married?" "Maybe your standards are too high." "I prayed for my husband. All you have to do is pray."
>
> Why can't people be more sensitive? Everything seems geared to couples in

> this world, even in churches: Valentine's Day banquets, Christmas banquets, overnight camping trips, retreats, etc. Everything revolves around husband, wife, parent, child, and teen.
>
> I know there are advantages to being single but if one more person tells me how cheap it is to live singly, I think I'll scream. They don't realize that we singles have just as many bills and payments as those who have husband, wife, or family.

We need to remember that God said it is *good* to be single.

Second, *accept singleness as a gift from God.* "Are you kidding? A gift from God? You bring me a man and then we'll talk about God's gift."

Paul said, "I would that all men were even as I myself. But every man hath his proper gift of God, one after this manner and another after that" (1 Corinthians 7:7). Sometimes God gives the gift of being single. Being married is a gift of God. Being single is a gift of God.

The *Living Bible* says, "God gives some the gift of husband and wife, and others he gives the gift of being able to stay happily unmarried." Jesus said, "For there are some eunuchs, who were so born from their mother's womb: and there are some eunuchs, who were made eunuchs by men: and there are eunuchs who have made themselves eunuchs for the kingdom of heaven's sake. He that is able to receive it, let him receive it" (Matthew 19:12).

People may be single for three reasons: physical, medical, or spiritual. It is clear that some of the greatest people who ever served God were single.

Third, *allow your singleness to become a source for growth.* It is not wrong to seek marriage, but it *is* wrong to let that search dominate your life. We must not make marriage the supreme goal of our lives, putting all our energy into finding a mate. Learn to be in God's will and be content. "There is something far worse than single loneliness and that is marital misery."

If God has a mate for you, He knows how to bring the two of you together. Don't take things into your own hands. Use this situation in your life as a time of growth. I think the young woman who wrote this note to me understood this truth. She wrote:

> Basically, I'm content at being single. I do hope the Lord has marriage in my future. Personally, I'd rather be married than single. But for now, I know the Lord loves me, and I know He has me single. Trusting in Him, waiting on Him and His plan is difficult. But I know that He is

> my rock, and that's more important to me than being married. Please pray that each day there will be more of Christ in my life.

Fourth, *activate your singleness for God.* A single person is free from the stress and strain of marital life, free to be devoted to God. I once heard that a man came to his pastor and said, "Pastor, my wife has left me." The pastor said, "When did it happen?" He said, "Well, I don't know for sure. It was sometime between Monday and Friday...I've been at church every night this week."

There's not a Christian man or woman who wholeheartedly loves God who doesn't struggle with priorities. How much time belongs to God? How much time belongs to others? How can all of us—single or married—put this together so there's a balance that's pleasing to the Lord? That's the kind of struggle we ought to be involved in. If we are married, the family is a priority in God's economy. Every child adds a new dimension of responsibility to our lives. I have no right to serve the Lord as a minister of the gospel and neglect my home and family.

But the thing Paul is saying is this: If you're not married and you don't have a family, you can give yourself totally to God without the pressure of those relationships. You can be totally consumed with serving

God in your life. If you are single you may say, "What in the world does that have to do with my loneliness?" Well, it has everything to do with your loneliness. People who are lonely as singles are people who are worrying about what isn't happening to them instead of what they should be doing to minister to others.

Here's a letter from another young woman. She said:

> Pastor, there have been many compensations for being single. How many husbands would have put up with the many midnight—or one-, two-, three-o'clock in the morning—phone calls I have received from my hurting friends. Many times I have gotten dressed and gone out in the middle of the night for a cup of coffee with a friend who was hurting.
>
> I'm so glad that God has used me in this small way. I place a high premium on my availability to other people. There are many verses that give me encouragement every day. A special one is Romans 8:32—"He that spared not His own Son but delivered Him up for us all, how shall He not with Him also freely give us all things?" Right now, His freely giving me all things does not include a husband. How dare I believe that God has made a mistake in His plan for my life?
>
> P.S. Please tell all the married people not

> to try to anticipate the will of God for their single friends by the compulsive need to matchmake.

It's okay to be single. If you are single, God has a special plan for you too. That plan includes reaching out and helping others. The answer to your need and aloneness—your feeling that you're not a part of what's going on—is not to wait until somebody gives, but to keep giving yourself. You'll discover that in serving God, it starts coming back to you and meeting the needs in your own life. (That principle works whether you're single or married.)

Fifth, *affirm your singleness with gratitude.* One thing I've learned in studying the subject of loneliness is that the supreme answer is a spirit of thanksgiving. It's hard to be lonely when you're thankful, because thanksgiving means taking spiritual inventory of your blessings. You realize that although you may physically be alone, God has done many good things to minister to your needs.

One young divorcee has found a way from loneliness to service, and describes her journey this way:

> Financial, emotional, and family stress are among the many areas the Lord has helped me to deal with as a single parent. A heart of thanksgiving is the answer to

overcoming depression and loneliness.

One particular area was extremely difficult for me to cope with. It is probable that other singles (particularly those who are widowed or divorced) experience this difficulty but are unwilling to talk about it with someone else, especially a pastor. Because sex is so personal, many people are hesitant to discuss it. The Lord has given me victory in this area, and I hope my sharing with you will enable you to counsel others.

My divorce was a painful time. During my ten years of marriage, my husband and I enjoyed a loving and fulfilling sexual relationship. At the time of our divorce, I felt an extreme need for physical contact but also felt that the Lord did not desire for me to seek a physical relationship. On my own steam, I tried to overcome my natural desires and I failed continually. My efforts produced only more frustration. After much struggling, I searched the Scriptures for a biblical answer to my frustration. Philippians 4:19 promises that my God shall supply all my needs. I had a *need* to be held and hugged. God created me; He knows me better than anyone. It was more than a desire...it was a *need.* I prayed and asked God to help me and to meet my needs.

The following morning I received a telephone call requesting me to teach the four-year-olds during the 8:00 o'clock

> hour. That Sunday morning was filled with hugs and kisses and an outpouring of God's love. The Lord has met my needs through the love of those children. Sunday morning is the highlight of my week.

Some parents are so concerned that their daughters or sons marry into high social standing that they will make any sacrifice (usually it's the sacrifice of their kids) to get them into marriage. The attitude that Paul is developing in this passage of Scripture is the attitude of praise for wherever we (or our children) are. At the end of the chapter he talks about being a widow and he says, "Maybe it's best if you not remarry. But praise God for it—be happy in that situation!"

I think what God is saying to us is that we can lift our eyes to heaven, and say, "Lord, I don't understand why I'm where I am. But I'm in Your will, I'm in Your plan, and I praise You for where I am. Use me right here to glorify Your name and to honor You and to be a blessing to other people and be thankful."

I also got a letter from a young man who understands where he is. He's a single who has internalized the truth of God's Word. He wrote:

> Let me share a few things that I believe were given to me by my Father in

heaven. He has taught me this in my experience as a single person.

Number one: Singles have a lot of love to give away, so give it! What I receive is usually somewhat proportionate to what I give. The biggest share of a blessing comes out of my giving, not out of my receiving.

Number two: The need to belong is responded to by my willingness to commit myself to something—to be vulnerable—to God, to a ministry, to a group, to a friend. I, as a single, often make the mistake of shying away from committing myself, and therefore I don't feel as if I belong.

Number three: Realize that loneliness is not always bad. In fact, on occasion it may be the very thing that draws me toward God. There is nothing that will bring me to my knees more quickly than feeling totally alone in a difficult circumstance.

Most of all, I need to be reminded that Jesus Christ has recognized me much more than I could ever realize, than I could ever deserve, than I could even know what to do with.

Christ recognizes me. If He died for me, if God sent His Son to pay the price for my sin, why wouldn't He be concerned about the well-being of my life, about whether I'm married or single?

God is concerned. He does love you. He wants to meet the needs in your life right now. He wants to be with you in your aloneness.

Lonely
Spouses

Chapter Four

Lonely Spouses

I have this hidden urge to see if there is some way I can get out of speaking on the subject of the family. I made a mental pact with myself a month ago, in fact, that I would never again speak on the family until my children were all grown. But some readers can't wait that long for what I need to discuss here, so I'm going to risk it.

I'm going to take great comfort in the fact that years ago when I was a seminary student, one of my professors told me that it wasn't necessary when you address a subject to be at the end of the road...just critical that you be somewhere on the road. I want to confess that I'm not at the end of this road, but I do think I'm making progress toward the goal that God has set before me in His Word.

Every day and every week, part of me struggles with the issues related to Christian family life. So, if I could say anything at all that will help us all feel better about these challenging truths, I would say that we need to become comfortable with the struggle because we're going to have it as long as we live. Sometimes we resent anything that upsets the equilibrium in our lives. We need to understand that God wants us to struggle. I don't mean in the bad sense, but in the sense that he wants us to deal with biblical truths in our real-life experience. We always seem to want to do the easy thing, but life is difficult. It takes struggle.

My strongest comments here will be directed at men. It's not that men are the loneliest. As someone has said, "They don't have the disease, they're carriers." Let me introduce this subject through some letters that were written to me some months ago by some very lonely married people.

The first is from a young wife:

> My husband and I have been married for almost two years. We became Christians after being married only six months. There was a dramatic change in both our lives. We were brought out of drugs, and more, by the Lord. But never has my husband given me any time.
>
> I love him, and I know he loves me, but I don't know how to tell him that I'm terribly lonely. I've asked him to spend time

> with me before, and he lovingly says he'll do better, but I never see him change. Before we got married, we used to sit outside and just talk until 3:00 or 4:00 in the morning. I enjoyed it so much and that's the big reason I married him. I had found a man who liked to talk to me about anything. And then as soon as we got married, we never seemed to be alone. He always had other friends around....
>
> I have my church family and they are all so special, but half of me is missing—even when he's home. We have a little girl, and I thought when we had her I wouldn't be lonely anymore. I was wrong. I need my mate, the other half of this union.

And here's another letter from a lonely spouse:

> Today you really struck a spot that's sensitive—I try not to dwell on it—loneliness in marriage. Both my husband and I are Christians. He is a good man, hard working, a good provider, not abusive, a fairly good father. My emotional needs are very rarely met because he is so hard working. It's the case of two people living parallel lives but never really meeting. We're both relatively well educated. He has heard and read a little about how a husband can create a good relationship with his wife, but it must all pass through him without making an impression. I try not to nag. Hurt is deep. I try not to think about it...is there some

> way I can get across to my husband that I need him—not what he does or earn?

The other side of the story came from this trucker:

> I am an over-the-road trucker. My wife left me several years ago and never came back. I had just gotten saved and began to apply biblical principles, but she thought it was too late. I remarried last December, and to be honest, I'm scared to death I'll do the same thing with my present wife.
>
> I tried, I really tried, but the pressure of being an over-the-road trucker is awfully great on a marriage. I had spent hours with my ex-wife trying to get her to talk—what were her needs, how could I meet those needs, but she would never open up.
>
> I get home, and I'm exhausted...I can't seem to move, and then there's the work at the church.

These people think their experiences are unique to themselves. Regrettably, however, what they write represents the experience of countless men and women. Perhaps as many as 90 percent of those who get divorces later confess that one reason for their ultimate marital breakup was the unbearable loneliness of living together but being far apart. The reasons for a man neglecting his wife and family, resulting in that kind of lonely feeling within her, are many-leveled; we can't chart them. But six or seven things happen as a result, and we can trace them.

First, many women respond to loneliness in their own home by going out and getting a job. Somehow that makes it more tolerable to live in the same house with a non-communicating mate.

Some women take their frustration out on their husband by joining a more or less militant women's group. They may become hostile toward men in general because they don't know how to deal with one man in particular (you know who). Some stay home and get depressed. Some crawl into a bottle, taking tranquilizers or alcohol or drugs. A growing number of women in our generation are following the pattern of men in earlier generations. If you do any reading in recent sociology, you know that a new phenomenon is runaway wives instead of runaway husbands. Women are getting fed up with it all. They leave and never come back.

What I'm talking about may be the best-kept secret in the Christian church. You see, when we come to church on Sunday, we come arm in arm. People look at us and say, "My, aren't they a lovely couple. They must have a wonderful life together." Yet we may have just had our worst fight ever in the car before we walked into church. The outer facade is never a very good indication of what's going on inside.

A poem by Edwin Arlington Robinson describes the secret loneliness of a man. It describes how carefully we camouflage what's going on inside of us so that others don't know.

Richard Cory

Whenever Richard Cory went down town
We people on the pavement looked at him:
He was a gentleman from sole to crown,
Clean favored and imperially slim.

And he was always quietly arrayed,
And he was always human when he talked;
But still he fluttered pulses when he said,
"Good-morning," and he glittered when he walked.

And he was rich—yes, richer than a king—
And admirably schooled in every grace:
In fine, we thought that he was every thing
To make us wish that we were in his place.

So on we worked, and waited for the light,
And went without the meat, and cursed the bread;
And Richard Cory, one calm summer night,

Went home and put a bullet through his
head.

(Morton Dauwen Zabel, ed., *Selected Poems of Edwin Arlington Robinson,* introduction by James Dickey, New York and London: Collier Books division of Macmillan Publishing Co., Inc., 1965, pp. 9, 10). Used by permission.

If I've learned anything about people, I've learned this: What you see on the outside may not be related to what's going on inside. Some of you reading about this sensitive issue of home relationships are hurting deeply in your heart, and not even your closest friend knows it. You haven't told anyone. Down beneath your facade is a person who cries out because of loneliness.

Some men have already determined that the pattern is set in their home. They're not going to change. That attitude represents male chauvinism in its truest sense. They're like the person described in a song called, "Put Another Log on the Fire." It goes like this.

Put another log on the fire,
Cook me up some bacon and some beans;
And go out to the car and change the tire,
Wash my socks and sew my old blue
jeans.

Come on, Baby,

You can fill my pipe, and then go fetch my

slippers,
And boil me up another pot of tea;
Then put another log on the fire, Babe,
And come and tell me why you're leavin' me.

Now don't I let you wash the car on Sunday?
Don't I warn you when you're getting fat?
Ain't I gonna take you fishin' someday?
Well, a man can't love a woman more than that.

Ain't I always nice to your kid sister?
Don't I take her drivin' ev'ry night?
So, sit here at my feet,
'Cause I like you when you're sweet,
And you know it ain't feminine to fight.

Come on, Baby,

You can fill my pipe, and then go fetch my slippers,
And boil me up another pot of tea;
Then put another log on the fire, Babe,
And come and tell me why you're leavin' me.

I know men like that, who, if God Himself came down and confronted them, wouldn't change. They don't want to. But if you're a man who cares that you continue to grow in an area which, in our culture, is a great struggle, then God has something to say to you.

A key verse in Ephesians 5 deals with our responsibility to dispel loneliness in our homes. It simply says this: "Husbands, love your wives, even as Christ also loved the church" (verse 25). Then Paul gives insight into the kind of love that will help us men know what God wants us to do in light of that responsibility. That love has five characteristics, five principles that God has given to us describing the relationship of Christ to the church as a picture of the relationship of a husband to his wife.

How did Christ love the church? However He did it, it's the way we are to love the woman whom God has given us to be our wife. First, *Christ's love was not romantic sentimentalism.* Jesus Christ loved the church realistically, and husbands are to love their wives realistically. One of the things I've learned in talking with people who are hurting in this area is that somehow they got off of "love for love's sake" and they got on to love for performance's sake. I used to give an excellent book on marriage, *One Plus One,* written by Tim Timmons, to all of the couples who got married in our church. It's the kind of a book that helps you understand what love really is and what it isn't. It teaches you that love is not based on what your partner does for you, nor on his or her performance. You love because God has given you this person.

One woman said, "I never feel that I measure up. It's never good enough, no matter what I do. So my relationship with my husband seems to be an up-and-down situation. If I'm good he loves me. If I'm not, he doesn't."

If Christ's love was conditioned like that, where would we be? He loves us in spite of who we are. That is one of the most overwhelming thoughts about the love of the Lord. He did not love me and then find out later what I was like. He loved me knowing all I would ever do to violate that love. He kept right on loving me, even to dying on the cross. It's that kind of love that is enjoined on husbands as we relate to our wives. Our love is a love that includes faults, failures, and all the unlovely and disagreeable elements that are a part of each of us. We love in spite of all that. It is the kind of love Christ had for the church, and it's that kind of love he expects men to have for their wives.

One problem a lot of young people face when they get married is that they have very unrealistic expectations. When they get into the situation they discover that it isn't what they thought it would be. I think those unrealistic expectations come from watching too much television and too many movies and from reading too many romantic novels. Have you noticed how we describe that whole process? We "fall" in love. When I hear that phrase, I always get a mental picture of walking down the street and falling into this huge gaping hole that envelops me. I fell in love. Some enchanted evening, across a crowded room, and you wake up the next morning and reality strikes hard.

Second, *Christ's love was sacrificial.* The Bible says that Jesus Christ counted the cost and gave Himself up for us. His love cost Him His life. So many people today are trying to find a relationship that doesn't cost anything. They want to receive but are never willing to give. Love between a man and his wife is a constant giving in, one to the other. Men love it when somebody preaches on the subject of the "submission" of the wife to her husband, but this very passage also clearly teaches mutual submission, one to another (Ephesians 5:21). There is a sense in which a "chain of command" in the home is reflected in Paul's words to his wife, but it's also true, and present right in this passage, that we are to be constantly submitting to one another. Marriages that work are marriages where mutual submission is a constant ongoing thing. It is a blending of ourselves together, the giving of ourselves, a determination that we will sacrifice whatever we have to for the sake of our loved one and our relationship.

It is interesting that the word *sacrifice* is made up of two Latin words, the first part meaning "holy" and the second part meaning "to make." It means we are to make holy at great cost the person whom we love. This means that if we are going to love our wives as we ought to love them, if that love is going to be the means God uses to dispel the loneliness of their heart, it will be a love that will cost us time and pleasures and ambitions and personal interests and friends. It will come to us at this level—that nothing takes priority over my wife, no matter how important anything else may seem to me. We will love sacrificially.

One woman said that when she asked her husband to spend time with the kids or with her, it was always tentative. If she got insistent about it, he said she was nagging.

> Honestly, I never wanted anything from him but himself, some part of him, and you can only ask for so long. There is a limit to how long you can be ignored and put off. You threaten to leave, without meaning it, until the day comes when you keep the threat. You consider all the unpleasant consequences until they don't seem all that unpleasant anymore. You decide that nothing could be more unpleasant than being alone and feeling worthless.
>
> You finally make your mind up that you

> are going to be a person with real worth as an individual. You assert your ego. You join womanhood again. That's what I did. I wanted to be more than a housekeeper, diaper-changer, and sex-partner. I wanted to be free from the deep bitterness and guilt that slowly ate at my spiritual and psychological sanity. Deep inside there was something making me not only dislike my husband but dislike everything he did and touched. His "I love you" became meaningless to me because he didn't act like it. His gifts were evidence to me of his guilt at not spending more time with me. His advances toward me sexually deepened the gap between us and frustrated us both.
>
> All I wanted was to feel that he really wanted to be with me. But no matter how hard he tried, I always had the feeling I was keeping him from something. Just once I wish he could have cancelled something for us instead of canceling *us*. All of a sudden I woke up one day, and realized I had become a terribly bitter person. I not only resented my husband and his work, but I was beginning to despise myself. So, in desperation, I left. I don't think he really believed I'd leave him. But I did.

That's scary. The amazing thing about such a relationship for a man who is totally inattentive to his wife is that sometimes he doesn't even know it. In one of his books,

Charles Swindoll comments that "marriages don't ever dissolve because of a blowout; they're always the result of a slow leak." Gradual dissipation. At the bottom of all of this is the fact that somebody somewhere in the relationship has refused to pay the price to keep the relationship alive.

Third, *Christ loved the church purposefully.* He loved the church in order "that He might present it to Himself a glorious church not having spot, or wrinkle, or any such thing; but that it should be holy and without blemish" (Ephesians 5:27). The purpose behind His love was the development of that church so that it could be all that He envisioned it to be. The purpose and motivation behind a man's love for his wife is that she might become all she should be as a person. It is quite opposed to the attitude of the man who tries to hold back any involvement or growth on the part of his wife. He is threatened by any of her gifts or abilities. He does everything he can to stifle her. He shuts her down as a person until she begins to doubt her own worth. The Bible teaches that a man who loves his wife will help her develop and mature until she becomes all she should be, all she can be. We men are facilitators to help make that happen in the plan of God.

Someone has adapted a song we often sing

and made it say what we're saying. It goes like this:

> Take my wife and let her be
> Consecrated, Lord, to thee,

That's not a bad motive, is it? "Lord, just help me to be, in the life of this woman whom I love, someone who encourages her to develop spiritually until she is all that she should be before You." Our love as men should be love with that kind of purpose.

Fourth, *Christ loved the church willingly.* Did God love us because we were lovable? Absolutely not. He loved us because in His divine prerogative He willed to love us. In time past, in eternity past, God said, "I will love," and He did. The commonly accepted idea about love today is that, if you don't feel like it, you can't do it. But that's totally apart from the truth. The truth is this: Feeling follows action; feeling follows the will. If I want to, I will. And when I do, my feelings follow.

Let me give you an illustration. I am a runner. Yet, to be very honest, no matter what all runners say, not one time have I ever run because I deeply wanted to. I never get up in the morning and think, "Wow, isn't it wonderful that today I can begin my morning by running four or five miles!" But when by an act of will I get this body going and start to run, the feelings begin to come. It feels good. And it feels most good when I get home and take a shower and am relaxed and know I've done the right thing. There's a euphoria about it that I can't express. Maybe it has to do with the fact that it's over.

So let me repeat. The Bible tells us that Christ loves the church because He wanted to, because He willed to. If husbands are to love as Christ loved the church, we are to love our wives because we want to, because we willingly choose to do the kinds of things our wife regards as loving. We're to take the actions that go along with love.

I was reading the letters to the churches in Revelation this week and something jumped out at me, probably because I was thinking about this. The church in Ephesus was told it had left its first love. Do you recall what the prescription was for the church that had left its first love? Go back and do the first works (Revelation 2:1-7). Let that grab hold of you. How do you recover a lost love? Go back to the beginning of the relationship and ask yourself, "What was I doing then that I'm not doing now?"—and do it. Take her some flowers. (You'd better be sure there's oxygen on hand, but do it) I guarantee she will like it. She'll feel better because you did it.

If you aren't all the way gone, if it's not too

late for you, if there's any hope at all, you'll discover all kinds of things that you feel better for doing too. The love that should be in your heart toward that woman will begin to develop according to your loving activities. We're responsible to be the leaders in love in our families. That's what it means to be the *head*—to be like Christ.

Last but not least, *Christ loved the church absolutely.* We are told to love our wives as we love our own bodies (Ephesians 5:28). For many years as I've studied this passage of Scripture and spoken on the subject to couples and young people, I always thought that this verse meant we are to love our wives just like we love or care about our own bodies. But that's not its full meaning. Paul is telling me that I am to love my wife because she *is* my body. She is part of me. When you get married, you become one flesh. Just as I will not neglect any part of me humanly that hurts, I cannot neglect any part of my wife that hurts. Together we share unity and oneness.

It's amazing to me how many women are hurt deeply whose husbands don't even know it. Sometimes a couple is seated in my room counseling with me about their problems and in a moment of great courage, usually because there is the supportive presence of the pastor, the wife blurts out something she's wanted to say for a long time. The husband will respond, "Why, honey, I didn't know you felt that way."

I pray every day that God will help me be sensitive to the hurts of my wife, be able to see when something is wrong that I need to be sensitive to—sense it on her face, or sense it in her spirit. Then I can reach out and touch her life as I ought to. That kind of caring will help dispel the loneliness that so many wives feel.

I am grateful for examples that God has brought into my life to demonstrate the importance of men learning to make family life a priority. One was Jim Dobson. When Jim came to grips with things going on in his life that were pulling him away from his home, he made some hard decisions. He cut out his speaking. He cut out his traveling. He decided to invest himself in things he could do at home so he could take care of his family.

I also remember one day when I was with Bill Gaither in his office. He was trying to get Jim Dobson to speak at one of his praise-gatherings, and he called him on the phone while I was there. When he hung up, he said, "Jim said he's no longer in the touring-speaking business. He's retired." After that, Bill and Gloria Gather started to make similarly tough decisions about their schedule. Two months in the year they would not accept any musical engagements. Bill totally reorganized his concert schedule in order to be home on certain weekend nights. I said, "Aren't you losing money?" "Yes," he said, "but it's worth it." I looked at his unbelievable pressure and schedule, and compared the meager things God has asked me to do, and thought, "Hey, if he can do it, I can." I'm still struggling, and sometimes it gets out of hand and I have to say, "How did this happen to me?" Now I pray I will never lose sight of this biblical priority.

Some of Bill's friends probably think he made a very bad business decision when he cancelled those Fridays and Saturdays. But I hope somewhere in eternity they have a chance to ask him that question again!

Lonely Seniors

My sister is fifty-nine years old...her husband of forty years left her to move in with a woman twenty years his junior. She feels life is totally over. No amount of support, counseling, etc., has helped her very much. She is living alone.

Severe loneliness can bring on illness and sometimes death. Why hasn't the body of Christ recognized the seriousness of this? Why not train young people to visit and help widows and orphans, the very isolated poor, the friendless?

I'm just past my eighty-second birthday. I live alone and because of illness I seldom get out to church services. It is not so bad in the summertime when I can be out in my yard for a while each day, but I am really a shut-in during the winter months. Sometimes at Christmas time, a small group of young people from my church will stop by and sing carols, maybe bring me a gift of fruit. Would you believe it, I can hardly find anyone with time to take me when I have a doctor's appointment. I pray for someone to come and help me in my loneliness here, and thus please the Lord and bring glory to His name. God answered my prayer last winter and sent a dear Christian friend once a week to wash and set my hair and prepare some foods that can be kept in the refrigerator for easy serving.

My husband went to be with the Lord several years ago. I can identify with the problems of loneliness, but the Lord is very precious. There is a dimension to my life that I never had heretofore. Many people confide their problems to me and ask me to pray for them. I teach Sunday school and am involved in other church activities.

Chapter Five

Lonely Seniors

An ancient king in a rage of anger once sentenced a faithful servant to death. Afterward, regretting what he had done, he summoned the condemned man and said, "In consideration of your long and faithful service to me, I have decided to let you choose the method by which you die." Without hesitation the servant replied, "Your Highness, I choose to die of old age."

Almost all of us, at least mentally, have made that choice. But, having decided to grow older, we don't deal with the aging process very well. We get caught up in a multifaceted quest for the fountain of youth. An elderly woman wrote to me about "the fear of losing authority and power of rank, and personal strength—and the 'pride of hearing.'...We are becoming gullible idolators of self-preservation," she said.

Certainly we sooner or later become preoccupied with aging. Geriatrics, the science or study of old age, is flourishing. That specialized branch of research studies the infirmities and maladies of the elderly and seeks remedies for them. Yet in spite of the innumerable brands of stimulants, hormones and pep pills and the longevity programs, people grow old.

Though we don't seem to know much more about handling the aging process gracefully, we have managed to prolong human life. Over 20 million Americans are sixty-five years old or older. There are over 22 thousand one-hundred-year-old-plus Americans. Medical science is saying that if it can learn how to treat arteriosclerosis effectively, by A.D. 2000 there will be 150 million Americans who are over sixty-five.

Since 1900, the number of people sixty years and older has increased four times as fast as those who are under sixty. At the turn of the century, there were 4.9 million Americans over sixty, and the average life expectancy at birth was forty-seven. Today 34 million Americans are over sixty, and the average life expectancy is seventy-three.

The trend toward a larger elderly population is expected to continue. Today one out of every seven Americans is sixty years old or older. When today's preschoolers become sixty, one out of every four may be sixty or older. "The U.S. population gets grayer every year."

Older people are among our loneliest citizens. Each year diminishes the number of their friends. Little by little their sense of self-worth and importance shrinks.

Some have tried to cope with the problem by organizing. Senior citizens' groups have grown up all over the country. The National Council of Senior Citizens now numbers over 3 million. The American Association of Retired Persons boasts a membership over 9 million.

One elderly protest group called the Gray Panthers is led by a spry woman now in her seventies named Maggie Kuhn. She and five friends, all retired church workers of different denominations, set up headquarters in Philadelphia's Tabernacle Church. Their basic goals are to develop a new lifestyle and base of support for the elderly. The Gray Panthers have a team of lawyers investigating old people's homes and lobbying in Congress for better legislation to protect the aged.

Kuhn has said: "Much of senility is not irreversible: It is induced by despair and frustration. Fixed retirement is dehumanizing. It shows how stupid our society is in making scrap piles of the elderly. We're not mellow, sweet old people. We've got time to effect change, and nothing to lose."

All of us who are Christians ought to have an interest in our responsibility both to old people and as old people. Older people suffer a kind of loneliness that is hard for younger persons to understand. Their loneliness usually stems from two things.

First, they have lost many of their contemporaries and loved ones, and they miss their fellowship. Second, they have a growing sense of uselessness as an individual. Many older people say to me, "I really don't know why I'm still alive in this world. What is there for me to do? What is my purpose in existing?"

Christians ought to know more about aging. The loneliness we face as we grow older seems to grip us with the same tenacity as it does those who are not Christians. We are not immune to the pain of aloneness when we lose a mate or close friend. We don't know how to deal with the growing feeling of unimportance. We don't seem to reflect the creative difference that growing older "in Christ" ought to make. Someone has said that "the devil has no happy, old people." Regrettably, the Lord doesn't have many either.

I have been looking around in my Christian

world for examples of men who were growing older with the outlook I anticipated Christians should have. Many negative, bitter individuals came to mind, along with a few gracious, positive models.

Then I began to look through the Scriptures to see if I could discover any biblical model of a man who grew old gracefully. One stood out, Caleb, a man from the tribe of Judah, the son of Jephunneh. Caleb first appeared in the book of Numbers as Judah's representative in the Kadesh-barnea caper (13:8). He and his friend Joshua brought back the minority report. The bad news: He was almost stoned by his hearers. The good news: He and Joshua were the only two of those who were adults at that time who were allowed to live long enough to see the Promised Land. As we begin to look at his story, he was eighty-five years old and about to experience the greatest moment in his life.

Caleb illustrates two important truths guaranteed to dispel loneliness in our senior years: You can accomplish life's greatest achievements in what we consider old age, and it is never time to retire from the Lord's work.

I see three principles emerging from Caleb's life that provide a path away from old age aloneness.

A. *Keep growing physically* (Joshua 14:10,11). Caleb felt as strong at eighty-five as he had at forty. A similar statement was made of Moses when he was a hundred and twenty. "His eye was not dim, nor his natural force abated" (Deuteronomy 34:7).

Most of the time we downplay the importance of the physical. The "outer man" hasn't gotten the attention he (or she) deserves. We are so into the spiritual that we have forgotten that the spiritual part of us needs a body in which to walk around. C. S. Lewis pointed to the critical relationship between soul and body when he wrote: "Our bodies and souls live so close together that they catch each other's diseases."

A lot of us work hard at ignoring the frustrations of growing older. One of the methods we employ is senior citizen humor. Somebody told me about a little girl who was sitting on her grandfather's lap. She looked at his white hair and wrinkled skin and asked, "Grandpa, did God make you?" "Yes, honey, He sure did," said her granddad. Then looking at herself, examining her smooth skin, she asked, "And did God make me?" "Absolutely." The little girl thought for a few seconds and then said, "Don't you think God's doing a better job than He used to?"

Another little girl asked her dad if he was

on the ark with Noah. When he said absolutely not, she wanted to know why he hadn't drowned. Because it is innocent, children's humor related to old age isn't so hard to take.

I'm not sure that other varieties of poking fun at the old are as palatable. For instance, have you heard these quips?

You know you're growing old when . . .

everything hurts, and what doesn't hurt, doesn't work.

you get winded playing chess.

you join a health club and don't go.

the only names in your little black book end in M.D.

your back goes out more than you do.

you sink your teeth into a steak and they stay there.

the little grayhaired lady you help across the street is your wife.

men, when you see a pretty girl walk by, your pacemaker makes the garage door go up.

And, I'm sure you've heard this folksong:

How do I know my youth is all spent?
My get up and go has got up and went.
My joints are stiff and filled with pain.
The pills that I take, they give me no gain.
I rub in the ointment, like fury I do.
Each pain when it leaves, comes back with two.

But in spite of it all, I am able to grin,
When I think of the places my get up has been.

Old age is golden I have heard it said,
But sometimes I wonder as I get into bed.
My "ears" on the dresser, my "teeth" in a cup,
My "eyes" on the table till I wake up,
Ere sleep comes each night I say to myself,
'Is there anything else I should lay on the shelf?'

—Author Unknown

It's all right to laugh at ourselves as the years begin to take their toll, but let's not use humor as a smoke screen to cover neglect and abuse of our body.

I visited Grace Village in Winona Lake, Indiana, a few months ago, and one resident took me down to her apartment. She showed me where she walks. Now at Grace Village you could run a 10,000-meter race and never go outdoors. It's such a spread-out facility with long hallways. She and a friend meet at a certain time each morning and they walk the halls of that place, up and down, from one end to the other, just as fast as they can walk.

Right on! That's what God intends us to do. These bodies of ours ought not to be allowed to deteriorate just because we're getting older. Most of it is in the attitude of our minds, not in the ability of our bodies.

Somehow Caleb kept "alive" physically, so that he was able to do at eighty-five what he did at forty. It's a reminder that decisions about health are fairly well established by the age of forty. Those decisions tend to set the tone for the rest of our lives. It also seems significant that most men and women start to give up on themselves at about that age.

Caleb, too, had every reason to do that. Think of it. Here he was, at the prime of his life, and what was his assignment? The desert. That's right, forty years in the desert with nothing much more exciting to do than bury the dead men who had chosen not to believe God.

While Caleb was engaged in that discouraging activity, Moses died, and Joshua was chosen to replace him. Caleb was passed over, and many men in his place would have given up on life right then and stopped caring about themselves. But Caleb didn't do that, and when God was ready, Caleb was prepared to walk on stage and play his part in the drama of Israel's relocation.

John Wesley was another Caleb-type. At eighty-five, he said he was not weary with travel or preaching—this, a man who had traveled over 250,000 miles on horseback, had preached over 40,000 sermons, and had written 400 books while learning and speaking ten languages. Wesley attributed his youthful activity at eighty-five to four things:

1. Exercise and a change of air
2. Never having lost a night's sleep on land or sea
3. Rising at 4:00 every morning
4. Preaching at 5:00 each morning for fifty years

When Wesley was eighty-six, he was annoyed that he couldn't write for more than fifteen hours a day. At eighty-seven, he was ashamed that he couldn't preach more than twice a day. And he confessed to a growing urge to lie in bed after 5:30 in the morning.

Our bodies are temples of the Holy Spirit, and there is no reason to believe we should stop caring for the temple after it reaches a certain age. So, do something to keep your body strong. If you can't run, walk. If you can't walk, shuffle. But don't give up on yourself physically.

B. *Keep growing mentally.* "Now therefore give me this mountain, whereof the Lord spoke in that day; for thou heardest in that day how the Anakim were there, and that the cities were great and fenced; if so be the Lord will be with me, then I shall be able to drive them out" (Joshua 14:21).

So many people stop dreaming. Their senior years are spent in loneliness and boredom because they've lost their dreams.

> Since I have retired from life's competition,
> Each day is filled with complete repetition.
> I get up every morning and dust off my wits,
> Go pick up the paper and read the o'bits.
> If my name isn't there, I know I'm not dead.
> I get a good breakfast and go back to bed.
>
> —Author Unknown

Caleb wasn't like that. He was by far the oldest, yet he asked for the toughest assignment. His contemporaries were dead and buried in the desert. The other men who were assigned an inheritance to claim were younger, but they weren't getting the job done. And Joshua was old, his days about gone, yet the thing God had instructed him to do wasn't getting done: "Now Joshua was old and stricken in years; and the Lord said unto him, thou art old and stricken in years, and there remaineth yet very much land to be possessed" (Joshua 13:1,13; 15:63; 16:10; 17:12,13).

Here we have clearly preserved for us the young Israelites' failure to do what had been commanded. "And there remained among the children of Israel seven tribes, which had not yet received their inheritance. And Joshua said unto the children of Israel. How long are ye slack to go to possess the land which the Lord God of your fathers hath given you?" (Joshua 18:23).

What they had failed to do, Caleb did. He was a tough-minded man in a weak-minded generation. He continued to be mentally what he had been at forty in Kadesh-barnea. He teaches us that it is our attitude of heart, not our activity or age, that determines whether we are young or old.

You are old at forty if you have stopped accepting challenges. If we look to the future only in terms of security, we have already set the stage of a lonely and discouraging lifestyle. In *There's a Lot More to Health Than Not Being Sick,* Bruce Larson says:

> ...A life of safety is no life at all, whatever your vocation. Still, we are programmed from an early age to start providing for a safe and secure future. Through pension funds and retirement benefits, we work toward removing all risk from our lives by the time we are 65. Yet in the three societies sociologists have studied where people normally live to 100 and frequently to 120, there is no special treatment for the aged. There are no retirement homes where people can spend their declining years playing shuf-

> fleboard. Scientists who have studied these societies have found they have nothing in common in terms of climate, diet, geography or life-style. But in all three places, the inhabitants are expected to live normal lives with no cushion for safety. They continue to work, tend fields and keep shops until they die at 100 plus. I am convinced that God never invented old age. Death is a gift, but old age is man's invention. It is a cultural blight in our life-time (Bruce Larson, *There's a Lot More to Health Than Not Being Sick*, Waco, TX: Word Books, 1981, pp. 75,76).

Caleb never stopped dreaming and growing, and God used him until his dying day.

C. *Keep growing spiritually.* Caleb said, "...I wholly followed the Lord" (Joshua 14:8). Three independent witnesses testify to the spiritual strength of this man. God said of Caleb at midlife, "But My servant, Caleb, because he had another spirit with him, and hath followed Me fully, him will I bring into the land whereunto he went; and his seed shall possess it" (Numbers 14:24).

At age eighty-five, Caleb himself looked back and evaluated. "Nevertheless my brethren that went up with me, made the heart of the people melt: But I wholly followed the Lord my God" (Joshua 14:8).

Moses added his testimony. "And Moses swore on that day, saying. Surely the land whereon thy feet have trodden shall be thy inheritance, and thy children's for ever, because thou [Caleb] hast wholly followed the Lord my God" (Joshua 14:9).

Caleb subdued and drove out his enemies, giants and all, because he wholly followed the Lord. He entertained no divided loyalties. He remembered God's promises. Three times in Joshua 14, Caleb referred to what the Lord had said about him. Those promises kept Caleb going during many years. He started believing God early in life and never stopped growing.

Remember the Kadesh-barnea days. The majority report came back from Canaan, a report filled with "giants," "strong people," "great walled villages," and ultimate defeat. But Caleb refused to give in to that pessimism and defeatism. He saw Canaan not as an obstacle but as an opportunity:

> Caleb stilled the people...and said, Let us go up at once, and possess it; for we are well able to overcome...the land is an exceeding good land...that floweth with milk and honey...neither fear ye the people of the land; for they are bread for us: their defense is departed from them, and the Lord is with us: fear them not (Numbers 13:30; 14:9).

That positive spirit kept him going strong. He was a brave man among cowards, an assured man among skeptics. His age changed; his attitude soared above circumstances.

Ours can too. I'm sure that's what Solomon meant in the book of Proverbs when he wrote that the beauty of old age is the gray head, and the hoary head a "crown of glory, if it be found in the way of righteousness" (16:31).

Lonely Servants

Here are the words of a preacher who, after eighteen years of ministry, quit and went into the business world, discouraged and defeated.

"Those years made me look and feel ten years older than I was. I had spent them holding people's hands, smoothing out countless interpersonal battles and church struggles, preaching how many hundreds of sermons, baptizing people, marrying them, burying them...as the church grew, so did the traffic to my office. I was not surprised at that, nor was I unaware of my calling, the demands I had to face in serving. But in all that time I could not find a confidant, someone who could simply listen and pray with me, not even my wife...most of the human problems I dealt with were confidential.

"While I struggled to find new and fresh sermon material, time for my own relaxed devotional life disappeared. When the church reached 1,200 members from the first 300, it was a sign of great blessing from God on my work. I accepted that and thanked God for it. But at the same time, I found myself even more lonely as the demands on my time tripled. My family was growing up and away from me. When I saw my children graduate from high school and then college, I realized I hardly knew them. I knew then I had to do something, though I was a little late.

"I concluded I could not abide that lonely road any longer...I knew I had to find some area of work where I could establish normal human relationships. Maybe I was just not cut out to be a leader, after all."

Chapter Six

Lonely Servants

All servants of God with a heart for people will sometimes experience the loneliness that comes in attempting to carry the burdens of others. More than once, they will be tempted to cry out as Moses did, "I cannot carry all these people by myself; the burden is too heavy for me" (Numbers 11:14, NIV).

There is no way to prepare a man or woman for that experience of aloneness. Each of us has to learn the hard way. If being a leader is defined as walking ahead of the group, that person is necessarily separated from the group. There is a sense in which "to lead" is to turn one's back on people.

The leader loses freedom in the service of others: promoting their interests, articulating their values, helping them to define their goals. At the same time, leaders are supposed to fulfill their own potential and not be absorbed by the group. Attempting to fill that kind of role often leaves leaders alone.

One missionary described leadership loneliness as:

> You feel alone in the task, realizing that there are no times of applause from anyone, no fitting into the social whirl of the good life at home, never really being a part of people in the normal concourses of life, because a missionary is, after all, a breed apart. That is the crushing load of the cross for me.

Another missionary said:

> The worst part of it all is that in twenty years of missions service I could never get close enough to anyone at home to really call them a friend. People would pray for me, as they said, as my name came up on the church's prayer calendar, but they could not pray for me as somebody they really knew. On deputation, I never confessed a human weakness. Nobody wanted to listen to that. It was embarrassing to them. A life of faith has no human frailties, so everyone assumes. To admit them was to destroy their ideal image of God dominating human chemistry. So they kept me above all that; they would not allow me to come down to where they were. I had to be on some level above them in order for them to maintain their trust in me as their missionary.

> Deputation is often a time of tears for me; it always has been. I desperately wanted people to accept me into their inner circles as a person, not a superhuman frontier warrior. I wanted to cry with them, laugh with them. I wanted them to do the same with me. Instead, we met, we talked, we passed each other. I did my act, they applauded, and that was that.

The New Testament provides insight into the loneliness of leadership. Demetrius, an ancient Greek literary critic, wrote, "Everyone reveals his soul in his letters." In the letters of Paul we have opportunity to look into his life and to view his solitude. I find his pastoral letters written to Timothy and Titus especially helpful. Those epistles show us the heart of the aging apostle.

Paul's second letter to Timothy is perhaps his most personal communication. Writing to his young friend who was pastoring in Ephesus, Paul was open about the loneliness he was experiencing.

1. *The loneliness of danger.* As he wrote, Paul was in prison in Rome. Outside in the streets, Nero's persecution was in full swing. Behind the facade of sophisticated Roman society lay total decay of morals and a growing disregard for human life. Suicide was rampant; men and women, tired of life, gave up and put an end to themselves. It was the

aftermath of the great Roman fire of A.D. 63, a fire that had burned half the city. Nero, responsible for that conflagration, had successfully blamed his crime on the Christians.

Some of those Christians were Paul's friends. Huddled in his cold cell, Paul died inwardly as the fate of Christian brothers and sisters became known to him. Some of them were covered with the skins of beasts and thrown to wild animals. Some were covered with flammable material and burned as human torches while Nero drove his chariot around the gardens indulging his warped mind in a carnival of fire and blood. Danger, terror, and persecution were in the air, and Paul, isolated in his prison room, could do nothing but grieve for his friends and anticipate an equally horrible end for himself.

2. *The loneliness of despair.* Off and on throughout his ministry, Paul had known the trauma of prison life. Most scholars believe he was now being held in the infamous Mamertine Prison. If they were correct, his cell would have been damp, reeking with pestilence, reminding him of the miseries of generations of condemned criminals. No wonder he asked for his coat (2 Timothy 4:13).

Paul knew there would be no escape from that cell apart from death. He had had his preliminary audience with Caesar and, although he had escaped death at that point (2 Timothy 4:16-17), it was just a matter of time. Public feeling toward the apostle and his converts was hostile. Allegiance to the Lord Jesus Christ was taken to mean high treason. The dark cloud that hung over Paul is felt in his words of resignation: "For I am now ready to be offered, and the time of my departure is at hand. I have fought a good fight, I have finished my course, I have kept the faith" (4:6,7).

Tradition has it that Paul was condemned to death and then beheaded as a Roman citizen on the Ostian Way about three miles outside the city. Eusebius, the Christian historian, says that Paul and Peter were executed on the same day, Paul by decapitation and Peter by upside-down crucifixion. Though we cannot validate the actual details of either death, we do know that Paul's second letter to Timothy was his last will and testament to the church. Shivering in his prison cell, he was writing with the knowledge that he would not write again.

3. *The loneliness of detachment and defection.* Paul's greatest pain was not the deprivations of his Roman cell, but his separation from caring companions. His anguish is seen as he wrote to Timothy about rejection: all

who were in Asia had turned against him, including Phygellus and Hermogenes (1:15). Demas had forsaken him, "having loved this present world" (4:10). Crescens had gone to Galatia, Titus to Dalmatia (4:10). Paul had sent Tychicus to Ephesus (4:12). Alexander, the coppersmith, had been on a rampage (4:14). Erastus had been left back in Corinth, and Trophimus was sick at Miletus (4:20).

Almost all of Paul's friends had seemingly evaporated at the time of his preliminary hearing before Caesar (4:16,17). We feel the pain in his words, "Only Luke is with me" (4:11).

Bishop Handley Moule wrote:

> I have often found it difficult to deliberately read these short chapters without finding something like a mist gathering in my eyes. The writer's heart beats in the writing. You can see his tears fall over the dear past and the harrowing present. Yet in spite of all of this, there is a noble solemnity. Here is a man on his way to death, and that he must say his words now or never, suffuses the whole composition. One moment he is strong with courage and the next he is tender as a child, when he begs his friend Timothy to come to him before winter, because he is so lonely.
>
> From his majestic survey of the past ("I have fought the good fight") and his con-

> fident anticipation of the future ("henceforth there is laid up for me the crown"), Paul returns in thought to the present and to his own personal predicament. For the great apostle Paul was also a creature of flesh and blood, a man of like nature and passions with ourselves. Although he has finished his course and is awaiting his crown, he is still a frail human being with ordinary human needs. He describes his plight in prison, and expresses in particular his loneliness.
>
> (Handley C. G. Moule, *The Second Epistle to Timothy, The Devotional Commentary Series*, London: Religious Tract Society, 1905, p. 16).

The desertion of Demas was obviously painful to Paul. Demas had previously been one of his close associates or "fellow workers." In the other two New Testament verses mentioning him, his name is coupled with Luke's (Colossians 4:14; Philemon 24). But now, instead of loving Christ's appearing as Paul did (2 Timothy 4:8), Demas had fallen in love with the present world system. The details of his defection have not been divulged; Demas may have been frightened by the reign of terror under which he was living.

A leader knows the biting hurt that comes when someone in whom he has invested much time turns away from the faith, and sometimes against the leader as well. I remember how I felt when a family I had personally won to Christ turned against me because of things said by a disloyal staff member. I don't remember, before or since in my life, experiencing any hurt like that.

Paul wrote in particular about the fierce opposition of a man named Alexander. This is probably a different Alexander from "Alexander the heretic" (1 Timothy 1:20) or "Alexander the orator" (Acts 19:33). The phrase describing his deeds might be translated "He informed many evil things against me." Some writers believe that Alexander was the informer responsible for Paul's second arrest. What Paul says here, however, is that he "strongly opposed our message" (2 Timothy 4:15, NIV).

Thinking back over my short ministerial career, I find my heart encouraged by the knowledge of the opposition to Paul. That kind of difficulty has triggered loneliness in me, too. (Paul's willingness to let the Lord reward the deeds of his opponents is a lesson I am still struggling to learn.) No leader who determines to walk the high road with his God will be able to escape that experience. I am comfronted at such times by the words spoken by John about Christ: "He was in the world, and the world was made by him, and the world knew Him not. He came unto His own and His own received him not" (John 1:10,11).

Dr. A. B. Simpson described his ministerial loneliness by saying he often was so misunderstood that he would look down at the paving stones in the street for the sympathy denied him elsewhere. Yet he knew at the same time that God was preparing him and molding him for a ministry of distinction in the future. Founder of the Christian and Missionary Alliance denomination, Simpson left behind him five schools for the training of missionaries, hundreds of missionaries in sixteen lands, and a large number of congregations in the United States and Canada who over the years have exerted a spiritual influence far beyond their numerical strength. "Often the crowd does not recognize a leader until he is gone, and then they build a monument for him with the stones they threw at him in life."

When Paul wrote in 2 Timothy about his first defense before Caesar, he was referring to the preliminary hearing that under Roman law proceeded the formal trial. According to law, Paul had the right to call a lawyer or witnesses. But not one of the Christians in Rome would speak in his defense. "No one stood with me," he wrote (4:16).

As Paul was called before Caesar, accused of disloyalty to the state and "atheism" (which to the Romans meant the refusal of idolatry or emperor worship), he was alone.

This was his Gethsemane. It could now be said of him as it was of his Lord, "They all forsook him, and fled" (Mark 14:50).

Yet in spite of difficulties and desertion by others, Paul also gives us insight into some of the encouragement we can feel during such hours.

Physical Encouragement

The part of Paul's loneliness that related to his body cannot be disregarded. His cloak, left with Carpus in Troas (2 Timothy 4:13), was an outer garment corresponding to an overcoat. Such cloaks in Paul's day were needed during the very cold winter months and winter was coming (verse 21).

Several commentators point out the historical parallel between Paul's imprisonment in Rome and William Tyndale's in Belgium nearly fifteen centuries later. In the words of Handley Moule:

> In 1535, immured by the persecutor at Vilvoorde in Belgium, he wrote not long before his fiery martyrdom, a Latin letter to the Marquis of Bergen, governor of the castle: "I entreat your lordship, and that by the Lord Jesus, that if I must remain here for the winter you would beg the commissary to be so kind as to send me, from the things of mine which he has, a warmer cap; I feel the cold painfully in

my head. Also a warmer cloak, for the cloak I have is very thin. He has a woolen shirt of mine if he will send it. But most of all, my Hebrew Bible, grammar and vocabulary, that I may spend my time in that pursuit" (Moule, *Second Timothy*, pp. 158,159).

Personal Encouragement

Our most obvious need in times of loneliness is companionship. The Lord is always with us, but most of us are like the little boy who was told that he shouldn't be afraid of the dark because the Lord was with him. "I know that," he replied, "but I want somebody with skin on." Paul was not different from us. He encouraged Timothy to bring Mark with him (the same Mark who had once deserted Paul but had now been restored). Paul missed him and wanted to see him once more.

Most of all, Paul wanted to be with Timothy again. "Do your best to come to me quickly" (2 Timothy 4:9, NIV). "Do your best to get here before winter" (verse 21, NIV). Paul seemed to know he would not survive the winter. He also knew that once winter came, Timothy would not be able to get through to Rome. It shouldn't be difficult for us to reconcile Paul's longing to be with Christ and his longing to see Timothy again. Both longings lie within the heart of the leader/servant.

Mental Encouragement

Paul mentioned to Timothy his desire for "the books, but especially the parchments" (4:13). The difference between the two was probably that the books were made of papyrus. Those papyrus rolls could have included any number of things, perhaps Paul's Roman citizenship papers, correspondence, or extra writing materials. The parchments may have been Paul's copies of the Old Testament Scriptures in Greek or the collected words of Jesus Christ. Paul desired to use his isolated hours redemptively. Studying what he accomplished during his imprisonments ought to make us all reevaulate our activity-packed schedules.

The loneliness of servanthood can often be a means to direct us into times of protracted study and meditation. Driven to this sometimes by my own loneliness, I have found great relief. The greatest challenge is to get over the initial emotional hurdle. At such times one doesn't feel like studying, reading, or meditating. But I find that when I take the step of faith to do what I know I should do, my feelings begin to change. I am buoyed up. My heart is encouraged.

Spiritual Encouragement

When Paul stood alone before Caesar, he was not really alone. "The Lord stood with me" (4:17). When it is possible for us to minister to lonely servants in some tangible way, we should never excuse ourselves by saying "Well, the Lord will be with them." On the other hand, the Lord's presence is anyone's greatest hope for lasting help. Paul said, "The Lord will deliver me...the Lord will preserve me" (verse 18).

As I am finishing this chapter, the Lord is allowing me to experience a time of intense loneliness. I have been reminded of some great promises in the book of Isaiah. They jump across the centuries to lift my spirit.

> Hast thou not known? Hast thou not heard, that the everlasting God, the Lord, the Creator of the ends of the earth, fainteth not, neither is weary? There is no searching of His understanding. He giveth power to the faint; and to them that have no might He increaseth strength. Even the youths shall faint and be weary, and the young men shall utterly fall: But they that wait upon the Lord shall renew their strength; they shall mount up with wings as eagles, they shall run and not be weary, and they shall walk and not faint (Isaiah 40:28-31).
>
> Fear thou not; For I am with thee: be not dismayed: for I am thy God; I will strengthen thee; yea, I will help thee; yea, I will uphold thee with the right hand of My righteousness (41:10).

> But now thus saith the Lord that created thee, O Jacob, and He that formed thee, O Israel, Fear not: for I have redeemed thee, I have called thee by thy name, thou art Mine. When thou passest through the waters, I will be with thee; and through the rivers, they shall not overflow thee: When thou walkest through the fire, thou shalt not be burned; neither shall the flame kindle upon thee. For I am the Lord thy God, the Holy One of Israel, thy Savior (43:1-3).

Those promises are found within a few lines of each other in Isaiah's prophecy. They are marked in red in my Bible. When I begin to feel discouraged and insecure, I turn there and reclaim the truth of God's never-ending presence in my life.

Lonely Sufferers

I am one of the loneliest people in this world. I only get to watch TV or listen to the radio because I have to stay home with an invalid husband. Seldom do Christians from our church come; they have their own problems. But I need to be with Christians. I have arthritis and a heart problem and I am legally blind. My husband has diabetes, is in a wheel chair, is almost totally deaf, and is legally blind. We often have real good days, and I praise God for them. I also can thank Him for our bad days. The devil is sure at work. I need lots of prayer.

Chapter Seven

Lonely Sufferers

It was when the lights went out and the room was suddenly plunged into darkness that the awful awareness came. The traffic of the hospital went on like an uncontrolled fever outside my door. But inside that room it became still, so still that you could sense, even believe, that the walls were moving and the room was becoming smaller.

"I was never a lonely person up till then. At least, I don't recall being lonely. But now I knew what it was. My family had gone home together to that familiar, safe place. But I was here alone, isolated, facing the uncertainties of what hospitals mean.

"Up to that moment I had joked and laughed with friends and family, because it all seemed like a lark. But now I knew. Suddenly I swallowed hard against the pressure in my chest. I was a little girl again, wanting someone to put on a light somewhere to cut the darkness, so I could get to sleep. I became terrified by the feeling. Sleep was a

> long time coming—hours of trying to push my mind off the emptiness, fear and darkness. The hospital slowly grew quiet, almost eerie, until there was only silence" (Quoted by James L. Johnson, *Loneliness Is Not Forever,* Chicago: Moody Press, 1979, p. 151).

People sometimes feel a special loneliness when they are called to go through an illness to face, in the intimacy of their own person, the unknown and frightening difficulties of that experience. C. S. Lewis wrote that God whispers to us in our pleasures, speaks to us in our conscience, but screams at us in our pain. Pain is a megaphone, Lewis said, that God uses to break into the deafness of our humanity, so that we will hear Him when He speaks.

In Psalm 116, David describes what happens when a person is sick . . . the characteristics of suffering. Notice first that he doesn't avoid the obvious, the pain. He talks about that discomfort without mincing words. It felt like the pains of hell, he said. "Pain grabbed hold of me; I couldn't get free from its grasp. I couldn't escape its torture." That pain brought despair into his life. "I found trouble and sorrow" (verse 3).

Despair developed into depression. The anguish of suffering causes tears to come. You feel as if you're losing your equilibrium, emotionally and physically. A forty-three-year-old man, taken to the hospital fearing he had cancer, described in present-day language what David was talking about in Psalm 116.

> "Everything about me was on a chart. I wasn't a name, except when they had to remind themselves who I was by checking my wristband. All of my body chemistry was on that chart. They knew what my blood was like, what pills I took and when, what my elimination habits were—they even knew through a monitoring system how I breathed, how my heart reacted to every move.
>
> "All of what was supposed to be *me* was on a sheaf of papers, but no one bothered to know me really. Here I was, a gregarious person who liked to laugh, and who cared. No one asked what made me cry, or if I liked to fish or go boating, or what sports I enjoyed, what food I liked to eat—none of the of that was relevant. I was not a human being, but an object for sticking and probing and testing and experimenting with. They stood over me and hummed or grunted or sighed or whispered off to one side. Seldom did anybody tell me what they were discussing. It all went on my chart, but none of it into my ears.
>
> "I was left to my own imagination of what was wrong—how serious it was—whether it meant a life of inactivity with

> my job on the line, becoming a burden to my family. After a while I sank deeper into the doldrums. I thought I was strong enough to lick anything that happened to me. But lying there day after day with my fears playing havoc with my mind and emotions, I was reduced to being a child.
>
> "One night I let the tears come. That was a shock, to realize I had come to a place of such total helplessness and despair and anxiety" (Johnson, *Loneliness*, pp. 153,154).

In his Psalm, David writes about the agony of being dependent. I suppose for men that's one of the most difficult parts of being sick. We think of ourselves as self-sufficient and independent and responsible for others, and all of a sudden we find ourselves in the hospital. At first it may seem kind of neat to be there, having someone caring for you like that. But finally you wish they would just go away. You don't want to see anyone who's coming to help. You want to do it yourself.

Someone has written that we spend our whole lives learning how to clothe ourselves sensibly, modestly, fashionably, attractively. Then we go to the hospital, and it all unravels in the mockery of that horrible contraption called a hospital smock. No matter where you sit down, it's still cold. Something about the way you are in a hospital tears your dignity apart. You can go in there the highest-class person in the world and in ten minutes you're as undignified as a baby—totally dependent. That's what David was talking about in verse 8. (This is not to say that hospitals don't care properly for people. It's just part of being sick.)

David goes on to describe the despondency that comes into the heart of a sick individual. He says, "I was greatly afflicted." And then he confessed to refusing to believe the truth. He said, "All men are liars. No on tells me the truth" (verses 10,11).

Some people in the hospital come to the place where they no longer believe they're getting the truth from people. They get so dependent that they can believe only *bad*. When someone comes and says, "Well, you're looking better today," they say, "No, I'm not. I'm not looking better. You don't tell me the truth. You're trying to keep me from the ultimate hurt." Despondency.

One of the problems with the Christian who suffers is the mental and emotional flogging they give themselves during the time they're ill. If there's any one question that people ask me when I visit them in the hospital or talk to them about their illness, it's this: "What have I done? Oh God, what have I done to be in this place? Why is God dealing with me in such a way? Why has God brought this sickness to my life? What does God have against me?"

And then they go back into their history and dredge up all the things they've done that they shouldn't have. They come to the conclusion that God is dealing with them harshly now because twenty years ago they were involved in *A,* ten years ago they did *B,* and so on. It all comes back. That's a message from Satan, you know; that's not from God.

A book by Joyce Landorf, *Mourning Song,* is the best book dealing with grief and death that I've ever read. She talks about some of the struggles people experience as a family when they face the pain of losing one of their family members. In one chapter she takes up this whole matter of remembering sin, using it to flog ourselves inwardly. We let ourselves believe that it's because of our sin we're in the situation we're in. A poem she quotes goes like this:

> I made a lash of my remembered sins.
> I wove it firm and strong, with cruel tip,
> And though my quivering flesh shrank from the scourge,
> With steady arm I plied the ruthless whip.
>
> For surely I, who had betrayed my Lord,
> Must needs endure this sting of memory.
> But though my stripes grew sore, there

came no peace,
And so I looked again to Calvary.

His tender eyes beneath the crown of thorns
Met mine; His sweet voice said, "My child, although
Those oft-remembered sins of thine have been
Like crimson, scarlet, they are now like snow.

"My blood, shed here, has washed them all away,
And there remaineth not the least dark spot,
Nor any memory of them; and so
Should you remember sins which God forgot?"

I stood there trembling, bathed in light, though scarce
My tired heart dared to hope. His voice went on:
"Look at thy feet, My child." I looked, and lo,
The whip of my remembered sins was gone!

(From *Her Best for the Master*, by Martha Snell Nicholson, published by Moody Press, Moody Bible Institute of Chicago, Copyright 1964. Used by permission.)

One of the most difficult things for us Christians (who have been taught from the Word of God about His goodness, blessing, and provision) is to accept the fact that sometimes for no reason other than our

benefit and His glory He allows difficult problems to come into our lives.

Charles Swindoll has written a book in which he talks about the four spiritual flaws—a parody, of course, on Campus Crusade's four spiritual laws. One of the four spiritual flaws he points out is this: God never allows problems to come into the lives of people who are living godly lives.

The Bible does not teach that. If you are suffering, if you are sick, if you're going through difficult times, it could be because of sin. That's a possibility. But it is probably because God loves you enough to want you to be all you can be, and He's taking you through some training to make you mature in faith.

The Bible says, "whom the Lord loveth, He chasteneth" (Hebrews 12:6). God's dealing in our lives is evidence of His love for us, recognition that we are His children. He is making us more like Himself.

A final characteristic of sickness seen in Psalm 116 is dread. Verse 3 speaks of the sorrows of death; verse 8 mentions death again. Never does a person with any kind of serious illness go into the hospital without death, the ultimate dread, being on his or her mind. We're put together in such a way humanly that when we get seriously ill, we carry it as far as we can—we assume the worst. David is doing that in this psalm. He is saying, "I'm going to die. Oh God, don't let me die."

All those feelings, written down hundreds of years ago, are as up to date as the closest hospital. Anyone who's suffered or been sick will tell you that most of the emotions described in this psalm have been in their lives in some way or another.

Bill Cearbaugh, a friend, wrote an account of his reflections on his wife's experience of loneliness during the months before she died from leukemia. With his permission, we are quoting a part of it here.

> Looking back on all of our situation, I especially remember when Rhonda got sicker and eventually had to go to the hospital. Unconsciously, I began becoming more and more removed from her. Often, as I went to the hospital thinking that I really wanted to serve her, I would let her try to sleep and not talk to her and be quiet. I isolated myself more and more by grabbing magazines at the lobby and and reading them, one after the other. Communication broke to the point where we hardly knew one another. She was getting so ill that she was finally put in a single room, by herself, and many times I would try to let her sleep by going to the lounge.
>
> I later realized that my motive probably

wasn't one of servanthood, but I just wanted to be removed from the situation. Because of her physical state, it became more and more difficult for me, as a husband, to really love her in the way I should. By then she had lost all of her hair, she had lost several pounds in weight, and she had been in bed so long that she had a number of bed sores. Her body was very white, with almost the look of death. Her eyes were sunken in and her face looked as though she had not eaten for several days. The taste buds of her tongue were beginning to drop off. A yellow film began to develop on her teeth, and her gums were bright red and highly infected. To complicate matters, the contraptions that were hanging out of her body—the intravenous tubes, the vacuum tubes drawing fluid from her lungs, and the oxygen tubes going into her nose to help her breathe—all made it very difficult for me to enjoy being around her.

I think the other reason I began withdrawing from Rhonda was that I became deeply concerned about our son's state. It became difficult to choose whether to be around John and make sure he was getting my attention or to be around Rhonda who desperately needed my attention also. I didn't realize I was violating a basic biblical principle at the time, that is that my spouse is a higher priority than my family. I can't even begin to imagine the loneliness that

> Rhonda must have experienced as I became more and more alienated from her. I think now of the emotions going through her heart, lying in bed in a dark single room, experiencing constant fever, unable to control her bowels and hearing the constant noise of the fluid being pulled from her lungs by the vacuum hose. The only interruptions were made by a nurse when she came to get the vital signs.
>
> I later found out from a friend who talked to Rhonda that Rhonda felt as though she had been left alone to die and no one really cared. Even though, every day, the family was around to help her and encourage her and share with her from the Word and pray with her, she still sensed inwardly that we were withdrawing from her.
>
> The remarkable part about this story, I think, is that though Rhonda had a deep growing relationship with Christ, and was continually developing it until the day she died, in the midst of that relationship she still experienced loneliness in her own life as she was dying.... Oh, that some day I won't be left alone to die.

But notice that the Psalm 116 does not leave us in despair. It tells us how to respond to that intense loneliness. We are to pray. "He hath heard my voice and my supplications" (verse 1). "He hath inclined his ear unto me" (verse 2). God is available. The psalmist cried to the Lord, and the Lord heard him. David said, "That's where I was. I cried for God. I reached out for Him." Three things happened. God heard. God helped. God healed.

A four-year-old girl got hurt, but she didn't cry for hours. She didn't cry, in fact, until her mother came home, and then she burst into sobs. Someone who was watching this, and had been aware of her injuries, said, "But why didn't you cry when you got hurt?" "Because there was nobody to cry to," she answered.

If you're a Christian, there's Somebody to cry to. That Someone is the Lord, and He hears. That's the first thing. God is not a dispassionate listener. He's an intense listener. In the aloneness you feel, you are not alone.

Second, David goes on to say that not only did God hear, but God helped him. "The Lord hath dealt bountifully with [me]" (verse 7). *Bountifully* is a wonderful word. It means that when I cry out to God, there is always more in His hand than I asked for to begin with. I don't understand that, but I believe it's true. It may not be exactly what you asked for, but it will always be better. It will always mean more in the viewpoint of eternity than anything you could hope for. God will help you.

Third, David says, "I cried and the Lord healed me." Verse 8 says he was delivered from death!

One summer while I was on vacation, I had the privilege of attending the Ocean City Bible Conference. On this particular Sunday, Anthony Campolo, an Italian sociologist and theologian, was talking about the common idea that it is the purpose of God to heal everyone from sickness. He described some of the hurt that such a philosophy brings on people. If they aren't healed, they feel it's because they don't have enough faith, or there's something wrong with them that God won't heal them.

Campolo went on the explain that it is obviously not God's desire or purpose to heal everyone in this world. But then he made an astounding statement. "But I want to tell you something, folks. It is God's purpose to heal everybody." He stopped.

I thought, "What's going on? He's just contradicted himself."

But he added, "He heals some here, and He heals some up there."

I couldn't help but wonder if that's why the verse that doesn't seem to fit in this chapter, verse 15, is here. It doesn't seem to belong in this context; you can't make sense out of its relationship to the other verses. It says,

"Precious in the sight of the Lord is the death of his saints." Ultimately He's going to heal them up there; make them all they never could be here. So when someone who is a Christian faces the ultimate, which is death—separation of the soul from the body, separation from this life into the next—God looks on that in a positive way. Now He can make that person whole and perfect.

David said, "I cried and He heard. I cried and He helped. I cried and He healed."

The end of the psalm is the therapeutic part for those who suffer the loneliness of sickness. Here are the conclusions of this sick man. He introduces them with a question, "What shall I render unto the Lord for all his benefits toward me?" (verse 12).

He answers with four "I will's." Four times he says, "This is what I will do." Number one: "I will remember my promises to Him" (verse 14,18). "I will pay my vows unto the Lord now in the presence of all His people." Have you ever noticed how many promises you make to God when you're hurting? "Oh God, get me out of this mess, and I'll do thus and this and all the rest." But isn't it surprising how quickly we forget what we promised to God when we were in trouble? David said, "I'm going to remember my promises to God."

Number two: he said, I will show my love

for God. In the midst of this situation, though I don't understand it at all, I'm going to love God. I'm going to express my love to Him.

Number three: he said, I will be thankful to God. "I will offer to thee the sacrifice of thanksgiving, and will call upon the name of the Lord" (verse 17).

Throughout this series on loneliness, we have focused on one word more than any other, the word *gratitude.* Can I as a lonely person be grateful? More than any other attitude, gratitude dispels the darkness of loneliness in a person's heart. In our experiences of suffering, the one thing that will help us more than anything else is to look beyond the difficulties and gratefully acknowledge that we have much in Christ Jesus.

Number four: "What shall I render unto God?" David said, "I will take the cup of salvation, and call upon the name of the Lord" (verses 12,13).

In the years of ministry God has given me I have learned that God can take tragedy and sorrow and use it as an arrow to the heart of a person who does not yet know Him—to cause that person to look beyond his or her own self and recognize that something is missing in that life. Facing sickness, tragedy, death, we can come alive spiritually.

Loneliness
in the
Bible

Chapter Eight

Loneliness in the Bible

What has happened to us? What has happened that human beings can no longer be near one another, even though we are right next to each other? When I opened the Bible and began to read with that thought in mind, I was overwhelmed at what I found. I discovered that although the word *lonely* or *loneliness* never appears in Scripture, the pages of the Bible are filled with illustrations about people who battled that disease.

The Reality of Loneliness

We can go back in the book of Genesis to a man named Enoch. The Bible says he walked a path quite apart from his contemporaries. In a wicked world, he stood out like a shining star on a dark night. The Bible says, "Enoch walked with God, and he was not, for God took him."

On the heels of Enoch came Noah, to whom God gave "absurd" instructions to build a boat where there was no water. For many years he worked at building that huge vessel. He was the subject of abuse by his contemporaries, but Hebrews tells us, "Noah walked by faith." He did what God told him to do, although he had to do it all by himself.

In Genesis 16 we read the story of a woman who experienced loneliness. Her name was Hagar. When Abraham's wife Sarah could bear him no children, she took Hagar, her Egyptian handmaid, and gave her to Abraham for a wife. Eventually, hostility between those two women grew to a boiling point, and Sarah banished Hagar to the wilderness.

As you read the story, you cannot miss the stress of her loneliness. She is all by herself—away from family and friends. There is no one there. Yet God met her at that time.

Walk with me to the mountain of Moriah. There Abraham trudged up to the pinnacle with his only son Isaac, to carry out a terrible instruction from his God: "Take that son who is the object of your love, and the hope and the promise of the coming nation, and put him to death." Abraham was so isolated in that experience that he could not even take his servants with him. He and his son went together alone to that mountain. And there God spoke to him redemptively.

Moses, too, was a man apart. We read his story in the book of Exodus. While working in Pharaoh's court he often took long walks by himself. On one of those walks, he came across an Egyptian who was fighting with a Hebrew. In anger Moses murdered that Egyptian, and as a result fled from Pharaoh into the wilderness. The next time we see him, he's wandering around on the backside of the desert, taking care of his father-in-law's sheep. Certainly during those years in his life Moses experienced loneliness.

David, the psalm writer, knew deep loneliness. We're indebted to him because he put into the words of his psalms the way a lonely person cries out to his or her Maker. How descriptively David expressed his solitude. "My days are consumed like smoke, and my bones are burned like glowing embers. I am like a pelican in the wilderness. I am like an owl of the desert. I watch, and am as a sparrow alone on the housetop" (Psalm 102:3,6,7).

David wrote, "Reproach hath broken my heart; and I am full of heaviness: and I looked for some to take pity, but there was none; and for comforters, but I found none" (Psalm 69:20). David expressed his loneliness in a way we can identify with.

Job stands out as the extreme and supreme Old Testament example of a lonely man. Nowhere did he find a receptive response. In the midst of his suffering, he felt that even God had abandoned him. He was an island among humankind, confronting the pain of his being.

When we leave the paths of the Old Testament and walk into the New Testament, we are introduced almost immediately to the disciples called by the Savior to help, encourage, and walk with Him in His earthly ministry. As we read the story, we can feel the growing emotions of fear and anxiety that well up in them as the Savior begins to talk about His impending death. Finally they begin to accept the fact that He really is going to die, that they are going to be deprived of His presence. They hurt with the misunderstanding that surrounds the loneliness of their knowledge.

Early in His ministry Jesus warned His disciples, "Behold, the hour cometh, yea, is now come, that ye shall be scattered, every man to his own, and shall leave Me alone" (John 16:32). The Savior, the Christ, felt loneliness. Not only did He experience loneliness when it came, but He knew intimately that it was coming—and all the anguish that went with the anticipation of it was His as well.

We follow Him in the closing hours of His life to the garden of Gethsemane. He took with Him three friends, and He asked them, "Will you stay here at the edge of the garden and watch and pray with Me?" Then He went into the garden and agonized over God's will in His life—the impending judgment of sin He would carry. When He came back to His friends, He found them asleep. You cannot miss the loneliness in His words. "What, could you not watch with me one hour?"

On Calvary our Savior experienced maximum loneliness. His friends had fled. One of His disciples had betrayed Him. Now, for a seeming eternity, even His Father turned away. In the agony of that hour, we hear the words of Jesus: "My God, my God, why hast thou forsaken me?" (Matthew 27:46).

The loneliness of that moment is beyond description, but it is the guarantee that Jesus is able to understand us in our battle with that enemy.

God's Comfort to the Lonely

Genesis 16 tells us that God met Hagar in the wilderness as she waited alone by the fountain of waters. Hagar was in the wilderness by herself, and when she realized that God saw her, she named a memorial to God's awareness of a lonely person.

Abraham's experience was something like Hagar's. When he was in the depths of his lonely obedience, God met him. At the exact moment when God knew that the testing had gone far enough, He broke in upon the silence:

> And the angel of the Lord called unto him out of heaven and said, Abraham, Abraham: and he said, Here am I. And he said, Lay not thine hand upon the lad, neither do thou any thing unto him: for now I know that thou fearest God, seeing thou hast not withheld thy son, thine only son from me. And Abraham lifted up his eyes, and looked, and beheld behind him a ram caught in a thicket by his horns: and Abraham went and took the ram, and offered him up for a burnt offering in the stead of his son (Genesis 22:11-13).

Notice the next phrase: "And Abraham called the name of that place, Jehovah-jireh..." (verse 14), which literally means, "The Lord will provide."

These two monuments in the Old Testament, Hagar's and Abraham's, testify to God's willingness to meet us when we hurt and are all alone. God also shows His care for us in the way He met with a number of other Old Testament people.

For instance, while Moses was alone in the desert, God spoke and revealed Himself to him through the burning bush. He said, "I'm here! And I want you to serve me." And He called him into service (Exodus 3:4).

Job, too, met God in his loneliness. In the midst of his tragic life, God spoke to him out of the whirlwind. No longer was God absent—He was present. Here are the words that Job spoke as the result of that experience: "I have heard of thee by the hearing of the ear; but now mine eye seeth thee" (Job 42:5).

David, who wrote about loneliness, is the same person who wrote, "The Lord is my shepherd; I shall not want.... Yea, though I walk through the valley of the shadow of death,...though art with me" (Psalm 23). He is the same psalmist who wrote Psalm 27: "The Lord is my light and my salvation,...the Lord is the strength of my life; of whom shall I be afraid?"

To the lonely disciples who mourned the anticipated absence of their Savior, Jesus said, "Let not your heart be troubled. Ye believe in God, believe also in me. In my Father's house are many mansions: if it were not so, I would have told you. I go to prepare a place for you.

And if I go...I will come again" (John 14:1-3). When you drop down in the text a few verses, you discover that on the heels of that promise for the future, Jesus did not neglect the present. He said, "I will pray the Father, and He shall give you another Comforter, that He may abide with you forever" (John 14:16).

The word *comforter* comes from the Greek word *paraclete,* meaning one who stands beside you. Jesus said "The Holy Spirit will come to stand by you."

The God who saw Hagar in the wilderness sees you. The God who provided for Abraham will provide for you. The God who revealed Himself to Moses will reveal Himself to you. The God who spoke to Job speaks to you today. The Shepherd and salvation of David is your Shepherd and your salvation. The Comforter that Christ promised to the disciples is your Comforter. He will come to you.

Most of all, the Christ who experienced ultimate loneliness will provide mercy and grace to help you in time of need (Hebrews 4:16).

Years ago, a philosopher named Seneca wrote these words in one of his epistles:

> For who listens to us in all the world?
> Whether he be friend or teacher, brother
> or father or mother, sister or neighbor,
> son or ruler or servant, does he listen?

> Our advocate, or our husbands, or our wives—those who are dearest to us—do the stars listen when we turn desperately away from man, or the great winds, or the seas, or the mountains? To whom can any man say, 'Here am I! Behold me in my nakedness, in my wounds, my secret grief, my despair, my betrayal, my pain, my tongue which cannot express my sorrow, my terror, my abandonment! Listen to me for a day, at least for an hour, or just for a moment.' Lonely silence...Oh, God, is there no one to listen?" (quoted by James L. Johnson, *Loneliness is Not Forever*, Chicago: Moody Press, 1979, pp. 137,138).

Jesus listens. Jesus will always listen. He is waiting for you to speak to him.